The New Leader's
100-Day Action Plan

THE NEW LEADER'S 100-DAY ACTION PLAN

How to Take Charge, Build Your Team, and Get Immediate Results

GEORGE B. BRADT

JAYME A. CHECK

JORGE E. PEDRAZA

WILEY

John Wiley & Sons, Inc.

Published by John Wiley & Sons, Inc., Hoboken, New Jersey.
Published simultaneously in Canada.

Requests to the Publisher for permission should be addressed to the Permissions Department, John Wiley & Sons, Inc., 111 River Street, Hoboken, NJ 07030, (201) 748-6011, fax (201) 748-6008, or online at http://www.wiley.com/go/permissions.

For general information on our other products and services or for technical support, please contact our Customer Care Department within the United States at (800) 762-2974, outside the United States at (317) 572-3993 or fax (317) 572-4002.

Wiley also publishes its books in a variety of electronic formats. Some content that appears in print may not be available in electronic books. For more information about Wiley products, visit our web site at www.wiley.com.

Library of Congress Cataloging-in-Publication Data:

Bradt, George B.
  The new leader's 100-day action plan : how to take charge, build your team, and get immediate results / George B. Bradt, Jayme A. Check, and Jorge E. Pedraza.
    p.   cm.
  Includes bibliographical references and index.
  ISBN-13: 978-0-471-78977-2 (cloth)
  ISBN-10: 0-471-78977-1 (cloth)
  1. Leadership—Handbooks, manuals, etc. I. Check, Jayme A.
II. Pedraza, Jorge E. III. Title.
HD57.7.B723   2006
658.4′092—dc22

                                     2005031906

Printed in the United States of America.

10 9 8 7 6 5 4

ACKNOWLEDGMENTS

We would need a separate book to acknowledge the people that have influenced our work on leadership transitions over the years. But we must acknowledge the contributions of our partners in PrimeGenesis up front. We started the firm in 2002 with an awareness of a real need and an idea and have managed to turn that into a set of tools and techniques that have helped people get on-board into new team leadership roles, deliver better results faster, and reduce their failure rate from 40 percent to less than 10 percent. Our partners' fingerprints are all over that success and all over the materials in this book: Ed Bancroft, Bill Berman, Meg Bradt, Bill Crain, Rob Gregory, Mark Hubbard, Mary Kaiser, Harry Kangis, Suzanne Pennella, Sandy Reeser, and Jim Singh. Think of them as co-authors.

We are indebted to our clients on a number of different levels. We are the first to admit that we have learned as much from them as they have from us. There are far too many individuals to name, and we have masked any story involving any of our clients, but those of you at the following firms know who you are: Ann Taylor, ARC, Barton Center for Diabetes Education, Boot Camps Unlimited and its boot camp attendees and partners, Citibank, The Coca-Cola Company, The Columbian Coffee Federation, Cornell University, Elizabeth Arden, FT Interactive, Goldman Sachs, Grey Advertising, Johnson & Johnson, Kinetic Concepts, Peter Kiewit, LexisNexis, Microsoft, Miller Brewing Company, MTV Networks, Neutrogena, Opus, Pepperidge Farm, Playtex, Prevention, Reebok, Royal Bank of Scotland, Sanofi-Aventis, Stora Enso, Stryker, 2 Spot Digital, Terex, T-Mobile, UBS, Unilever, The United Way, The YWCA.

Finally, abounding gratitude to our editor Richard Narramore, our agent Jim Levine, and our friend and sometimes skipper Philip Ruppel, who introduced us to both of them. Without those three, this book simply would not exist.

CONTENTS

PART III
WHAT LEADERS KNOW

APPENDICES
TEAM, MARKETING, AND STRATEGIC PLANNING TOOLS USEFUL ACROSS STEPS

Executive Summary

AN "ON-BOARDING" PROCESS FOR LEADERS AT EVERY LEVEL

Whether you are a veteran CEO taking the reins of your next organization, or a new frontline supervisor, *The New Leader's 100-Day Action Plan* will help you manage your leadership transition so you can take charge, build your team, and deliver better results faster than anyone thought possible. This matters because 40 percent of leaders going into new roles fail in their first 18 months. (Yes, 40 percent!)[1]

What do these leaders not know or see? What do they not do? Why are they not able to deliver? In most cases, they miss one of the crucial tasks that must be accomplished in their first 100 days. Some don't understand the impact of their early words and actions and inadvertently send their new colleagues all the wrong messages. Some focus on finding a new strategy, but fail to get buy-in and fail to build trust with their new team. Some do a lot of work without accomplishing the one or two things that their bosses are looking for. No leader wants this to happen.

We have designed this book as an action plan, with a timeline and key milestones you need to reach week-by-week, to set you and

---

[1] The 40 percent failure rate comes from a study by the Center for Creative Leadership as cited by Anne Fisher in "Don't Blow Your New Job," *Fortune*, June 22, 1998. Brad Smart cited a failure rate of 50 percent in his book *Topgrading*, Upper Saddle River, NJ: Prentice Hall, 1999. *Human Resources* magazine cited a Right Management Study on August 21, 2004, that indicated the 2004 rate was 35 percent. Leadership IQ published a study September 20, 2005, suggesting that the failure rate is 46 percent at 18 months. So, 40 percent is still looking like a good benchmark.

your team up for success in your first 100 days. These are distilled from insights gleaned from working with clients of our consulting firm, PrimeGenesis, whose sole mission is to coach executives moving into new leadership roles. You will find our clients' stories throughout this book (masked to preserve confidentiality). We hope you will find this to be a practical handbook that helps you know what you need to know, see what you need to see, and do what you need to do to deliver success quickly and decisively.

Over the years, we have noticed that many new leaders show up for a new role smiling, but without a plan. Neither they, nor their new companies have thought things through in advance. On their first day, they are welcomed by such confidence-building remarks as: "Oh, you're here. . . . We'd better find you an office."

. . . Ouch!

Thankfully, some enlightened companies have a better process in place. If you are lucky, you will be associated with a company that actually puts people in charge of preparing for a leader's transition into a new role. Imagine the difference when a new leader is escorted to an office that is fully set up for her, complete with computer, passwords, phones, files, information, and a 30-day schedule of orientation meetings.

Better. . . . But still not good enough. Even if the company has done this for you in advance, if you have waited until this moment to start, you are already behind, and you have stacked the odds against yourself. We have tested and evolved PrimeGenesis' on-boarding methodology in many different environments, with all types of leaders. We have found there is a huge difference between the leader who has a plan, hits the ground running, and makes an impact on his first day on the job, and the leader who waits until Day One to start planning. Clients who have used our methods have been able to deliver better results faster. And they've reduced the rate of failure of leaders going into new roles fourfold—from the 40 percent we quoted to well under 10 percent.

Here are our three most important recommendations for leaders going into new roles:

1. *Take charge of your own "on-boarding" process.* It should include discrete steps structured and driven by you over time. (Mirroring the steps in this book.)

2. *Get a head start before your first day.* Day One is a critical pivot point, and a major opportunity to accelerate progress—

if you can hit the ground running. A little early momentum goes a long way.

3. *Think team.* In the first 100 days, it is essential to put in place the basic building blocks of a high-performing team. You will fail if you try to do everything yourself without the support and buy-in of your team. As a team leader, your own success is inextricably linked to the success of the team as a whole.

Consider the example of the Puritan Foods team at Procter & Gamble, which in six months, accomplished more than anyone thought possible. The new team leader was given a budget to test market Puritan Foods. A budget, but no team. He had to recruit volunteers to work on the project in their spare time. The good news was that this meant that everyone who worked on the project was doing it by choice. Their mandate was to get a set of new products into test market as quickly as possible to learn about those products and their consumers.

The team was comprised of people from product development, finance, sales, market research, and marketing. They identified outside suppliers to create, manufacture, and distribute the products and to manage in-store tests. They rented a townhouse as a base for the team in the test market, established their own sets of communication and decision practices, laid out their plans and timelines. And they went to work, picking up some early wins along the way and adjusting team members' roles as appropriate.

The result was that they went from "Make it happen" to 12 new products on the shelf in under six months—faster than anybody thought possible at Procter & Gamble at that time. Four of the 12 test products were expanded into successful businesses. Furthermore, what the team learned about health-conscious consumers made a big impact both on the balance of the Puritan business and on other Procter & Gamble businesses. Better than anybody thought possible!

How? Why? In essence, the leader and his team did everything they were supposed to do in the first 100 days. The new leader had a plan for hitting the ground running. He got started working with key people before Day One. And he focused on getting the right people on his team, aligned around one burning imperative throughout. The details of how you can do that fill the rest of this book.

How to Quickly Build a Highly Effective Team or Organization: The Core Principles

We are going to take you through a step-by-step on-boarding process that can be followed by leaders at every level to deliver better results faster. Paradoxically, the best way to accelerate a transition into a new leadership role is to pause long enough to think through and put an on-boarding plan in place.

Here are the three main conceptual frameworks underpinning the on-boarding plan in this book (Figure 1.1):

1. High-performing teams and organizations are built of people, plans, and practices aligned around a shared purpose.

2. Tactical capacity bridges the gap between strategy and execution, ensuring that a good strategy doesn't fail because of bad execution.

3. Five building blocks underpin a team's tactical capacity: a *burning imperative*, key *milestones*, *early wins*, getting the right people in the right *roles*, and shaping the *culture* with an ongoing communication plan.

FIGURE 1.1   Core Frameworks

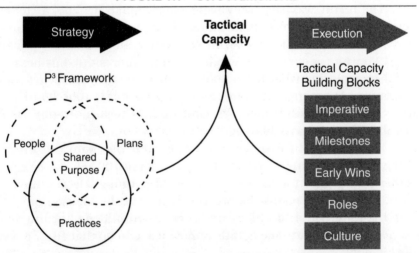

People-Plans-Practices—P³

An organization or a team's performance is based on aligning its people, plans, and practices around a shared purpose, what we call P³. This involves getting the right *people* in the right roles, getting clarity around the strategies and action steps included in *plans*, and getting *practices* in place that enable people to implement the plans in a systematic and effective way.

Tactical Capacity

Tactical capacity is a team's ability to work under difficult, changing conditions and translate strategies into tactical actions decisively, rapidly, and effectively. It is the essential bridge between strategy and execution. In contrast to other work groups that move slowly, with much of the direction and most of the decision making coming from the leader, high-performing teams empower each member to come up with and quickly implement critical solutions to the inevitable problems that arise on an ongoing basis. They build on strategy and plans with the right people and practices to implement ever-evolving actions that work.

You have seen this yourself. You have been on teams with members that operate in loosely connected silos, incapable of acting without specific direction from above. They may know the strategy. They may have the resources they need. But any variation or change paralyzes them.

In contrast, a great example of tactical capacity at work was how NASA team members came together during the Apollo 13 crisis. Right from "Houston, we've had a problem . . ." the team reacted flexibly and fluidly to a dramatic and unwelcome new reality—a crippling explosion en route, in space. They went beyond their standard operating procedures and what their equipment was "designed to do" to exploring what it "could do." Through tight, on-the-fly collaboration, the team did in minutes what normally took hours, in hours what normally took days, and in days what normally took months. This was critical to getting the crew home safely.

If you're lucky, you've been on teams where actions and results flow with great ease, where team members know what is really required and support each other in making those things happen. Those teams have tactical capacity.

Here's a mouthful of jargon, but it's important: Tactical capacity is built on the alignment of people, plans, and practices around a shared purpose. As the new leader, it's your job to orchestrate this alignment. You must convince key people to turn a shared purpose into a burning imperative and get widespread buy-in for it by communicating constantly with the team and broader organization. A burning imperative is the antidote to silos and departments that don't cooperate. Tactical capacity is not only about the team being able to respond quickly to changes in external circumstances, it also is about team members working well with each other in support of the team's burning imperative.

Building Blocks of Tactical Capacity

The good news is that you, as a leader in a new role, can build tactical capacity into your team quickly by implementing five building blocks, each of which is described in its own chapter in this book:

1. Get buy-in for the one *burning imperative.*
2. Use key *milestones* to drive team performance.
3. Invest in *early wins* to build team confidence.
4. Get the right people in the right *roles.*
5. Shape the team *culture* with an ongoing communication campaign.

The NASA team dealing with the Apollo 13 crisis got each of these five building blocks in place, allowing it to react with tactical capacity of the highest order:

1. The team's mission changed from "going to the moon to collect rocks" to the one *burning imperative* of "get these astronauts home alive." This was galvanizing enough (as a burning imperative must always be) to transcend all petty issues and focus everyone's efforts.
2. The team's *milestones* were clear: turn the ship around, preserve enough energy to allow a reentry, fix the carbon monoxide problem, survive the earth's atmosphere, and so on.
3. The carbon monoxide fix kept the astronauts alive temporarily, and was the *early win* that made the team believe it could get the crew back to earth safely. It gave everyone confidence.
4. Everyone was working with the same end in mind. But they were working in different and essential *roles.* One group figured

out how to turn the spaceship around. Another group fixed the carbon monoxide problem. Another dealt with the reentry calculations. And the spare crew did whatever it took. They were all working together, without getting in each other's way.

5. The *culture* had been strong. But everyone's words and actions reinforced the message that "failure is not an option" throughout the rescue mission.

Even though you're unlikely to jump into a situation as urgent as Apollo 13, in today's environment, almost all leadership transitions are "hot landings" where you must hit the ground running to have a chance of succeeding. Very often you will need to fix something, fast. Sometimes you and your team may have to react that quickly to changing situations. Sometimes you will have more time to plan. Fortunately, this is the case in most on-boarding situations. You will have at least a few days to create an on-boarding plan—if you get a head start.

The 100-Day Action Plan

Here are the steps in our on-boarding process (and, conveniently, this book's chapters).

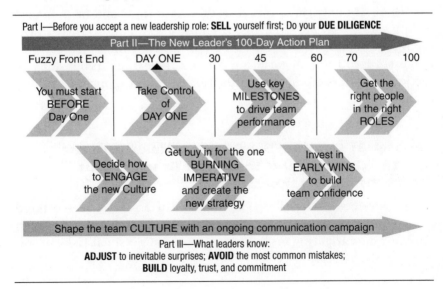

An Overview of the 100-Day Action Plan

The New Leader's 100-Day Action Plan is divided into three parts:

> Part I describes things you need to do before you accept a new leadership role.
>
> Part II is the heart of the 100-Day Action Plan. It picks up right after you accept the job and runs through your first 100 days.
>
> Part III adds things you need to keep in mind throughout your first 100 days (and throughout your career as a leader).

Here are the main points, chapter by chapter.

Part I   Before You Accept a New Leadership Role

Chapter 2: *Sell* Yourself First: How to Negotiate for a Leadership Position

You cannot turn down a job you have not been offered. So first put all your energy into getting the job offer. To that end, remember that there are only three real interview questions and be prepared to talk about your (1) *strengths,* (2) *motivation,* and (3) *fit* with the organization and the position. Then, when things get serious, make sure you are negotiating all the important dimensions of the job, well beyond just compensation to role responsibilities and authority.

Chapter 3: Do Your *Due Diligence:* Make Sure the Job, the Culture, and Your New Boss Fit Your Strengths and Weaknesses

Once you've been offered the job, and only after you've been offered the job, make sure it is right for you. This involves choosing between options and mitigating organization, role and personal risks by answering three questions:

1. What is the organization's sustainable competitive advantage?
2. Who had concerns about the way the role was designed; and what was done to make them feel better about it now?
3. What, specifically about me, led to your offering me the job?

Part II   The 100-Day Action Plan

Chapter 4: You Must Start *before* Day One: Especially with Your Boss and Key Stakeholders

How do you take charge, build your team, and get great results . . . faster than anyone thought possible? Cheat. Seriously, create time by starting earlier than anyone thought you would. Key steps for this golden time between acceptance and start include:

- Identifying key stakeholders up, across, and down.
- Managing personal set-up.
- Conducting prestart meetings and phone calls.
- Gathering prestart information and learning.
- Planning your first 100 days.

Prestart meetings and phone calls are a great chance to jumpstart relationships and get at learning, expectations, and implementation.

Chapter 5: Decide How to *Engage* the New Culture: Assimilate, Converge and Evolve, or Shock

Be "choiceful" about how you enter an organization, using an ACES model to determine whether you want to assimilate, converge and evolve, or shock it at the start. You need to make this choice before you walk in the door because it will change your approach to Day One.

Chapter 6: Take Control of *Day One*: Make a Powerful First Impression

Everything communicates. And, at the start of a new role, all communication is magnified. Thus, it is essential to be particularly choiceful about everything you do and say and don't do and don't say—and in what order and to whom you do or say them. That's why you, and only you, have to be in control of the first impressions you make on and around Day One.

Chapter 7: Get Buy-In for the One *Burning Imperative* and Create the New Strategy (by Day 30)

The burning imperative is the cornerstone of tactical capacity. Everything pivots off a team's mission, vision, and values. For this and the new strategy to drive everything everyone actually does every day, they must be truly shared. Get them created and bought into early on—even if they're only 80 percent right. You and the team will adjust and improve along the way. But don't let anything distract you from getting this in place and shared.

Chapter 8: Use Key *Milestones* to Drive Team Performance (by Day 45)

The real test of a high-performing team's tactical capacity lies in the formal and informal practices that are at work across team members. Tactical capacity requires that significant leeway be built into those practices. Use a flexible team-based milestone management practice to build in nuances, insight, monitoring, and collaboration.

Chapter 9: Invest in *Early Wins* to Build Team Confidence (by Day 60)

Early wins are all about credibility and confidence. People have more faith in people who have delivered. You want your boss to have confidence in you. You want team members to have confidence in you and in themselves. Early wins fuel that confidence. To that end, identify potential early wins by day 60 and deliver them by the end of your first six months.

Chapter 10: Get the Right People in the Right Roles (by Day 70)

Support people who are in the right role and performing well.

Move people who are in the wrong role and performing poorly.

Invest in people in the right role but who are not performing well.

Evolve to new roles people in the wrong role and performing well.

Chapter 11: Shape the *Culture* with an Ongoing Communication Campaign (throughout Your First 100 Days)

Map the existing culture and coalitions. Then deploy an all-out, multimedia communication campaign over an extended period to shape and evolve the culture to where it needs to be. Doing this right requires a great deal of effort. The payoff is both huge and lasting.

Part III   What Leaders Know

Chapter 12: *Adjust* to the Inevitable Surprises

It is essential to monitor the situation over time. Identify and classify surprises' impacts as major or minor, enduring or temporary, and be ready to react as appropriate. For major, enduring changes, redeploy and/or restart. For major, temporary events, follow the basic flow of prepare—understand—plan—implement—revise/prepare. And manage communication relentlessly.

Chapter 13: *Avoid* the Most Common Mistakes

Avoid stepping on seven common on-boarding landmines:

1. *Organization:* Lack of a winning strategy; or inability to implement that strategy
2. *Role:* Expectations and resources or key stakeholders not aligned
3. *Personal:* Gaps in individual's strengths, motivation, or fit
4. *Relationship:* Failing to establish/maintain key relationships up, across, or down
5. *Learning:* Situation, customers, collaborators, capabilities, competitors, conditions

6. *Delivery:* Failing to build a high-performing team and deliver results fast enough

7. *Adjustment:* Not seeing or not reacting to situational changes

Chapter 14: *Build* Loyalty, Trust, and Commitment

Great leaders focus more on their followers than on themselves. The more they sacrifice for the benefit of their followers, the more loyal their followers are to them. Leaders like that are around today. They are easy to spot. They are the ones people are following.

Make This Book Work for You

By now you should understand that there is a better way to manage transitions than just showing up on Day One and doing what "they" tell you to do. Furthermore, there may be a better way for you to tackle this book than just starting on page one and reading straight through until you lose steam. You might want start with the 100-Day Checklist at the end of Chapter 4. You might want to begin with the chapter summaries. Or you may prefer to read straight through. Use the different elements in the way that work best for you. We have designed this as a flexible handbook: practically oriented, with ideas, examples, tools, forms, and checklists in the book, with easily downloadable and printable versions of them online.

The rest of the book will help you put this methodology into practice. As you set out to do that, understand that we have a bias to push you to do things faster than others would expect. This timetable is based on the needs of our clients who typically are in demanding new leadership roles, who need to meet or beat high expectations; but it may not be appropriate for your situation without some customization. We're going to present you with options and choices. But you're in charge. We wish you success in your new leadership role. We hope this book will help you and your team deliver better results faster than anyone thought possible!

PART I

BEFORE YOU ACCEPT A NEW LEADERSHIP ROLE

CHAPTER 2

Sell Yourself First

HOW TO NEGOTIATE FOR A LEADERSHIP POSITION

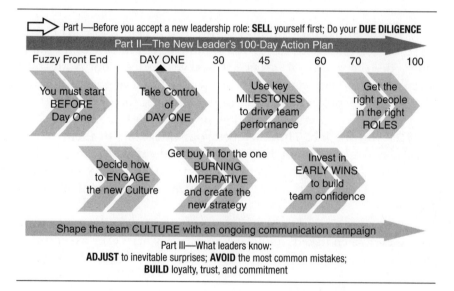

Champion athletes know that the race begins long before the starting gun is fired. This is almost a cliché, but it is startling how rarely executive leaders really make the most of the time *before* they start a new job.

So here's our first tip: Your new assignment started as soon as you learned you were a candidate. Treat it as such. Get up early. "Go to work." Spend the time and effort that you would if you had already started the job. You wouldn't walk into a presentation to the board of directors unprepared, would you? Each interaction with the people who will be involved in hiring, evaluating, and working with you should bear the marks of careful and thoughtful preparation, delivery, and follow through. You are making many critical first impressions. Patterns of perception and behavior are being set. You should be the one to script them. Carefully plan and prepare for each of your meetings during the hiring process.

Here are two thoughts about the time leading up to a job offer:

1. You cannot turn down a job you have not been offered.
2. There are only three real interview questions—ever.

You need to do two things before you accept a job: (1) get offered the job and (2) decide if you should accept it. Don't mix them. Don't do them out of order. If you've figured out your own strengths, motivations and "fit" criteria, if you've gotten in front of the right people at the right organizations, then you're selling. Everything you do in the interview process is designed to get them to offer you the job. This includes your questions to them. Those questions are not about helping you decide if you want the job. They are about helping them decide to offer it to you. Secure the offer. Then, after you've got the offer, figure out if it's right for you.

There are only three real interview questions. Every question you've ever been asked, and every question you've ever asked in an interview is a subset of one of three questions. The questions are:

1. Can you do the job?
2. Will you love the job?
3. Can I stand working with you?

Or, alternatively:

1. Strengths
2. Motivation
3. Fit

That's it. Those three.

The good news is that now all you have to do is to prepare three answers in advance and you're ready for any interview:

Question 1: What are your strengths? (Strengths)

Answer: Prepare three situation/action/results examples that high-light your strengths in the *areas most important to the people interviewing you.*

Question 2: What are you looking to do? (Motivation)

Answer: Position *the role* you are applying for in terms of your values and what you like to do.

Question 3: What sort of people do you like to work with? (Fit)

Answer: Position *the organization* you're interviewing with in terms of your values, and people with whom you like to work.

The bad news is that it is going to be a lot more work than you might think to prepare these in advance of each interview. Interviews are exercises in "solution selling." They are not about you. They are about your ability to solve the organization's and interviewer's problem. That's why motivation is about how your values and what you like to do *fit with the role.* That's why you need to high-light strengths in the areas *most important to them* and why you must *position their organization* in terms of your values. Thoughtful preparation can often be the single deciding feature between a yes and a no. This is tricky stuff. It is worth the investment of time.

A new leader and a new team are being put together to solve a specific problem or address as specific need or goal. These may or may not be fully understood by the parties to the project, and they may or may not be fully articulated to you. In many cases, organizations think and learn about what they want as they conduct the hiring process. You can have more of an impact on what the organization needs and what the job should be at this point than you realize. Very often, the winning candidate is the one who, acting as a management consultant, helps the decision makers and team members get a better sense of what the problems, or needs, really are, and conveys a sense of confidence that under her supervision the right things would get done.

But return to the three interview questions. Since you have done your homework, all you have to do is figure out which question you are really being asked, answer the question stated and bridge to the real question. In general, we recommend your answers first address your strengths, then motivation, then fit. A skillful interviewee is able to transition smoothly from the topic at hand, whatever it is, to the key points they want to cover, and to a discussion about how/why there is a good fit.

For example:

"Tell me about yourself."	*Great.* This common but somewhat dauntingly open-ended question sets up all three of your answers. The joking-chatting time is over; you've been given the reins for a bit. Be ready to lead. Lead with your strengths and let the interviewer guide you to motivation and fit.
"What do you know about me/us."	*Motivation.* Prove that you cared enough to do some homework. You should show that you know, or have been able to surmise, something about their strengths and motivation, which you can then lead to yours and to the vital question of fit.
"Tell me about your career transitions."	*Motivation.*
"Tell me what you did at . . ."	*Strengths.*
"Tell me about your favorite boss."	*Fit.*

Strengths, motivation, fit. You've most likely been involved in hiring a new leader and know that those involved in the decision can have wildly different ideas about what to look for. If you're lucky, you've had the experience of a "great candidate" emerge from the process. And if you're luckier still, this person did in fact end up being what people had hoped.

How does a "great candidate" emerge and why? What usually happens is that the candidate somehow manages to hit the right buttons for two or more people in the process, and these people in turn begin to influence the process in his behalf. And how does that happen? Chance? Possibly, but skill is likely also involved. The candidate is able to present strengths and motivation in such a way as to touch on the "right buttons" and to get the discussion onto the question of fit. How do skillful candidates do this? One standard technique is to structure the interview as an exchange where as much information is being given as is being put out. In fact, as in any selling situation, there needs to be a sense of an even flow back and forth of queries, expressions of interest and enthusiasm, and so on.

Great job candidates are able to foster a lot of enthusiasm in the people who are interviewing, and that enthusiasm in turn gives the candidate a lot of insight, which in turn allows the candidate to sell himself more effectively. And how do you foster enthusiasm? By presenting yourself with confidence and professionalism, certainly, but also by being enthusiastic. Great candidates create a sense of enjoying the interview process, of really liking to talk about work and management and opportunities. This is not to be confused with an attempt to behave like a cheerleader with pom-poms. A skillful interviewer helps set up the conditions where "things that matter" are being discussed. What's important to you, what's important for them, and inside of that, what really motivates you and what really motivates them. Each of us, in our own way, will find a way to communicate that enthusiasm compellingly.

So, in a nutshell, come prepared, present with confidence, be enthusiastic (talk about what really matters), brim with a sense of possibility and opportunity. These will get you an inside ally quickly, which is often the way to getting the opportunities you want offered to you.

Again, that's easy to say, but can be harder to do. How can you get yourself to where these things come naturally for you? We have developed a tool for you, the "Five-Step Career Plan."

Tool 2.1 Five-Step Career Plan

George has been sharing this particular tool with people for over a decade. It has some surprising uses that will come up throughout this book: It helps people looking for a new job; gets people to think about whether their existing job is the right one for them, and so on. Go to the performance versus potential matrix in Chapter 10 and you'll see how this tool will help people self-select out of roles that are wrong for them.

The point of this tool is to provide a quick and effective way to understand what makes you tick professionally and to make important career decisions. If you're like most people, you actually get tired when you think about making important career choices. It is tiring. It makes you nervous. It makes you feel somewhat inadequate. Or frustrated. Try to relax and let yourself go through this process. Capture that wonderful sense of excitement that you have when you feel important things are possible. How do you do this? Well, start by asking yourself what's important. Deceptively simple. Very productive. And write your answers down. Do not just run through the questions impressionistically, "I would probably say x or y." Make the commitment of writing it down and building your own plan. (Remember this for all the tools in this book. Writing choices down makes them more real.)

Here is the outline. We'll guide you through each point in greater detail in the text that follows. You will be building a response to each of these elements. Use your language, your terms. Build a profile and plan that provides you with some sense of satisfaction when you read it.

There is a downloadable, printer-friendly copy of this tool (and many other tools in this book) at www.primegenesis.com/tools.html. Some will find it easier to write things down on the form you print out than to write in the book. But it's your book. Do what you want. (Unless you're in Japan. Don't write in books there. Or at least don't let any of your Japanese teammates see that you wrote in the book. They'd think less of you.)

Let's walk through the main steps.

First of all: Take this seriously. There's no kidding anybody here, no pretense, no right answer, no wrong answer, no one answer. Just ask yourself the questions truthfully and see what you come up with. Don't just read through this and think about what you would say if you were asked these questions. Ask them, really, and write down your answers! Put them down for a while, mull over it, and come back and see what else comes up:

- *Likes/dislikes:* This is your raw data. Try to come up with how you actually feel, rather than how you think you should feel. Go through your past activities and jobs and lay out everything you liked and didn't like. This is about specifics, not generalities. I liked planning, thinking, getting a sense of accomplishment, working with people I liked, having some freedom, being rewarded for performance. I liked the support system in a big company, the short commute, having weekends free, and so on. I did not like it when I was pushed too hard, or when there was an overly critical or competitive atmosphere, when I could not take Sunday off, when things did not work right, when my colleagues let me down, feeling like a company of second-class citizens, and so on.

- *Ideal job criteria:* With these things in mind, lay out your ideal job criteria. If you could wave your magic wand, what would that dream job look like? Explore what it is about these criteria that are meaningful or important to you. Test, challenge, shape your answers. Nothing about this should be rote or removed from you.

- *Long-term goals:* Next, think about your long-term goals. Define these any way you'd like: in three years, in five years, before you retire, and so on. What do you want to achieve? Think directly about your professional life and about your personal life, and especially about the ways these are connected. Throughout all this you should be connecting your strengths, motivations and criteria for fitting in. You may feel you have a good sense of these before you start. Or you may feel that these are too removed from the practical job at hand. Either way, go through this exercise, and open yourself to a genuine question: What matters to you?

- *Options:* Our experience has been that the idea of options triggers widely different responses in people. When it comes to big choices, some people are somewhat overwhelmed. They become oddly passive, or even fatalistic. "What will be will be." And once things play out, "Well, it was meant to be." We urge a strong position in the opposite direction. With all due respect to those who consult astrologers and believe in fate, we are convinced that the mind-set that generates a sense of possibilities, of options, is the mind-set that *creates* opportunities and fosters success. We can not emphasize this enough. There is no point where this approach is more important than when you are about to take an important assignment.

  Here's a fundamental truth we believe in: Options energize potential. As much as possible, create parallel options. Real ones. Even if option two is not nearly as attractive as the main option at hand, the fact that there a viable alternative is absolutely crucial to your success with negotiating and setting up the first option. If at all possible, you want to have at least two job offers from which to choose at the same time.

- *Choice:* If you've done your homework, you will have at least two real options to choose from when the moment comes to make a decision. Go back to your list of ideal job criteria and long-term goals. Look at your options. Think through what the options are really likely to bring you. This is where you compare options by weighting your criteria and evaluating each option's results.

- *Gut check:* There's a hidden step. Once you've made your choice, write it down and go to sleep. If you wake up in the morning feeling good, then you have probably made a good decision. If you wake up in the morning with your gut indicating that you have made a mistake, you lied to yourself. Most likely, where you lied to yourself was on the weightings of your ideal job criteria. It's okay to lie to yourself—just as long as you have a mechanism to catch it. Your gut is that mechanism.

This is perhaps easiest to understand with an example. Imagine your only criteria are money and location. Job A is in a great location and pays $150,000/year. Job B is in a less exciting location and pays $200,000/year. If you chose job B and wake up with your gut screaming at you, you probably weighted money too high and location too low. Change the weightings until they spit out the choice you really want to make.

Negotiate for Success

You got the offer! Congratulations! You're done! Accept and move forward. Right?

Wrong! Don't relax yet. There's often a real sense of urgency on the part of the hiring organization to move from offer to acceptance to start as quickly as possible. It's a huge trap. The goal is not to start quickly and provide those involved in the hire with a sense of relief that their part of the project is over. The goal is to set things up for a successful outcome over the long term. Even with the initial offer in hand, there are things you need to do to set yourself up for this success. As any mogul skier knows, if you're focusing on the bump you're just going over, the next one can throw you off. Look ahead.

You may have to shape that offer to turn it into a recipe for success. First you *sell* to get an offer. Then you *negotiate* to get the right offer. Then you do a thorough *due diligence* to decide if you should accept. It's important to do these in sequence so that you don't muddle your thinking or send mixed messages. With the offer in hand, selling is over. Let's deal with negotiating here. We'll tackle due diligence in the next chapter.

You certainly want to negotiate a win-win package factoring in all the different forms of short-, mid-, and long-term compensation, benefits, termination rights, and the like. It's equally important to negotiate the details of the role and responsibilities, expectations and authority. There are generally more dimensions open to negotiation than is readily apparent. Take a hard look at the role's responsibilities and relationships. Make sure they line up with appropriate authority and resources. If there's a mismatch, negotiate to correct it here or pay the price later. While it's great to get any offer, it may be just the next step toward crafting the right offer.

Finally, a word about negotiating. Many people find negotiating for job terms unpleasant, possibly even distasteful, and it makes them nervous. We have found that in the face of this nervousness, people resort to uncharacteristic behavior. They become oddly passive. Or oddly aggressive, playing out some imagined role from the Godfather. We could write a separate book about negotiating. For now, suffice it to say that it can and should be done in a positive, constructive, collaborative atmosphere and tone. It's about clarifying needs and desires, and energizing both parties. Successful negotiations typically leave both parties energized, and there is no situation where this would be more important than in negotiating for a new job responsibility.

Tool 2.2—Negotiating Worksheet

Once you've been offered your new position, the negotiating begins. To ensure that you address all the issues that are essential to your success, you can follow our six step process on negotiating.

1. *Plan:* My/their needs and concerns (dimensions of negotiation)
2. *Get started:* Areas of agreement
3. *Clarify positions:* State, support, listen
4. *Find alternatives:* Consider other paths, options
5. *Gain agreement:* Proposals, concessions, summarize, test agreement
6. *Implement:* Communicate, deliver, monitor

Plan

There are two parts to this, mapping out the needs and concerns—yours as well as theirs—across the critical dimensions of negotiation. Your dimensions fall out of your ideal job criteria and long-term goals. It's important to know what you want and what you're willing to give up to get it. To complete this process, identify your walk-away, minimum, expected, and opening points for each critical dimension for you and for them.

> For you:
>
> *Walk-away* is the minimum you'll even begin to talk about. If the other party opens with something below that point, you walk away without even countering.
>
> *Minimum* is the minimum acceptable.
>
> *Expected* is where you think a deal will be done.
>
> *Opening* is what you'd say first if asked.

> For them:
>
> *Walk-away* is the maximum they'll even begin to talk about. If you open with something above that point, they walk away without even countering.
>
> *Maximum* is the maximum acceptable.
>
> *Expected* is where they think a deal will be done.
>
> *Opening* is what they'd say first if asked.

For example, on the dimension of base salary, there is a deal to be done. You, the new leader are expecting a base salary of

You:	< $80,000		$105,000		$125,000		$140,000	
	Walk-away		Minimum		Expected		Opening	
	▼		▼		▼		▼	
		▲		▲		▲		▲
		Opening		Expected		Maximum		Walk-away
Them:		$100,000		$110,000		$130,000		$150,000

$125,000, but would take as low as $105,000. The company is expecting to pay you $110,000, but would pay as much as $130,000. Thus, there is a deal to be done somewhere between $105,000 and $130,000.

The dimensions are important. The more dimensions you can negotiate on, the more room there is for give and take. For many people, a $100,000 straight salary is not as good as a $90,000 salary with a $10,000 per year travel allowance. Or a salary of $90,000 and a bonus of up to $25,000. As the level of the role increases, the degrees of freedom on negotiations increase as well. A good way to learn what's possible is to pull recent employment contracts for senior leaders of the company off the web.

One executive got bored with his retirement. He applied for and was offered a job in a consulting group with compensation of a straight salary. His response was "That's much less than I've been used to earning. But, given my stage in life, I could be happy with that annual salary if you gave me 20 weeks vacation a year." And they did.

We've used a base salary example because it's easy to illustrate. You'll want to map all the important dimensions of short-, mid-, and long-term compensation, benefits, termination rights, role, responsibilities, expectations, and authority out on similar scales.

Sell Yourself First— Summary and Implications

Get the offer first.

Prepare for an interview by being ready to sell your strengths, motivation, and fit.

In the interview, make your points fully, but succinctly, and then be quiet and listen.

Negotiate all the important dimensions.

We will talk about turning down the wrong job in the next chapter.

Downloadable TOOL 2.1
Five-Step Career Plan Worksheet*

1. Make a list of your likes and dislikes (include elements like past activities, jobs, situations, lifestyle, etc.).

_____

_____

2. List your ideal job criteria in each of these areas:

Compensation (reward, recognition, respect, fit with strengths and life interests)

_____

_____

Employability (learning, development, resume builder)

_____

_____

Meaning in the work (impact on others, interesting work, activities, enjoyment, values)

_____

_____

Life interests:

• Application of technology: How things work, how to improve

_____

_____

• Quantitative analysis: Gravitate to numbers

_____

_____

• Theory development, conceptual thinking

_____

_____

(continued)

Downloadable TOOL 2.1   (Continued)

- Creative production: New elements of business, products

_____

_____

- Counseling and mentoring: Helping people working under them

_____

_____

- Managing people, relationships: Motivate, organize, direct others

_____

_____

- Enterprise control: Running things, "owning" transaction

_____

_____

- Influence through language and ideas: Persuasion, communication

_____

_____

Share in shaping destiny (influence, being informed)

_____

3. Identify your long-term goals.

_____

_____

4. Build options—Broad range of options in parallel: Understand in detail.

_____

_____

5. Choice—Evaluate options versus criteria.

_____

_____

Downloadable TOOL 2.2
Negotiating Worksheet*

(For each dimension)

My opening: _____

My expected: _____

My minimum: _____

My walk-away: _____

Their walk-away: _____

Their maximum: _____

Their expected: _____

Their opening: _____

Get Started

Negotiations are always easier if you can start by agreeing. Find the areas that you agree on and discuss those first.

Areas of agreement:

_____

_____

_____

There's a framework for areas where there's a difference as well:

Areas for debate:

1. State your position.

2. Support your position with other information.

3. Listen to the other person's position and probe for understanding. Don't challenge at this point. Just seek to understand.

(continued)

Downloadable TOOL 2.2   (Continued)

Areas for debate:

_____

_____

Find Alternatives

Then look for ways to meet everyone's needs. Often this involves bringing another dimension into the picture.

_____

_____

Gain Agreement

Again, there's a process for managing this:

1. Receive and make proposals.

_____

_____

2. Receive and make concessions on different dimensions.

_____

_____

3. Summarize the situation.

_____

_____

4. Test agreements.

_____

_____

5. Circle back to concessions until there's a complete agreement.

_____

_____

Implement

Implementing is all about following through. You need to do what you say you're going to do. You need to communicate steps along the way. You need to deliver. And you need to monitor all the parties so you know they are delivering as well.

CHAPTER 3

Do Your *Due Diligence*

MAKE SURE THE JOB, THE CULTURE, AND YOUR NEW BOSS FIT YOUR STRENGTHS AND WEAKNESSES

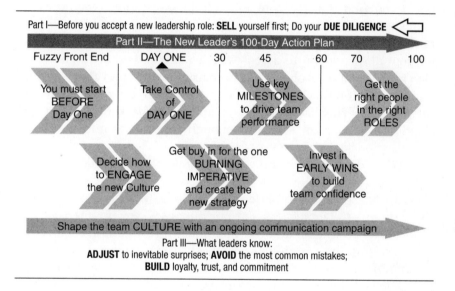

Part I—Before you accept a new leadership role: **SELL** yourself first; Do your **DUE DILIGENCE**

Part II—The New Leader's 100-Day Action Plan

Fuzzy Front End   DAY ONE   30   45   60   70   100

You must start BEFORE Day One

Take Control of DAY ONE

Use key MILESTONES to drive team performance

Get the right people in the right ROLES

Decide how to ENGAGE the new Culture

Get buy in for the one BURNING IMPERATIVE and create the new strategy

Invest in EARLY WINS to build team confidence

Shape the team CULTURE with an ongoing communication campaign

Part III—What leaders know:
ADJUST to inevitable surprises; **AVOID** the most common mistakes;
BUILD loyalty, trust, and commitment

Why do due diligence? Due diligence is about understanding and mitigating risk. To make sure that you and your new team will be able to make a difference and exceed expectations, you need to have a good sense of what things could go wrong—for reasons that have nothing to do with you, your team, or your combined efforts—that prevent you from achieving your goals. We recommend that you assess the risks from three vantage points: *organizational, role,* and *personal.* Do not underestimate the importance of this. It is going to be far less painful to turn down the wrong organization or the wrong role than it is going to be to try to salvage an unsalvageable situation. You need to get these three elements out of the way before you accept the job so you can concentrate on other, more rewarding things down the road.

How do you do due diligence? This might seem daunting at first, but you are actually in a privileged situation. Obviously, you can draw on public information about the industry, the company, and so on. But since you and the company are in a process of mutual exploration, you are in a position to meet with and talk to people who will help you get better information about what's really going on. If you find that the company is reluctant to give you access to people and information, you are already learning something important about the company. They are asking you to make a commitment without allowing you to assess whether the fit is truly a good one. Don't be afraid to probe. What is their concern? Can they see your point of view on this? There will be times when, for various reasons, information truly is confidential and must be kept so. But you should be able to get access to enough people and information to build a good sense of the broader picture.

When do you do due diligence? In a way, you start doing it right away and you never stop. A great leader is always reassessing the risks to her business practice and looking for ways to minimize these threats to her success. For our purposes, you do intensive due diligence once you get an offer and make sure you have acquired as much relevant information as possible by the time you need to make a commitment. So it will overlap with some of your negotiating.

Michael Ovitz's experience as president of Disney is an example of how *not* to do due diligence. As revealed in court and depicted in Bruce Orwall's *Wall Street Journal* article on the subject, Ovitz, his boss, and the organization at large had completely different views of what Ovitz was supposed to accomplish, where he was supposed to focus, and who was to report to him.[1] As Orwall points out, "even before the deal was announced, it had gone sour." CEO Michael Eisner quickly went from thinking he'd found his eventual successor to describing Ovitz as a "psychopath," "untrustworthy to everybody," and "totally incompetent." While Ovitz's $140 million severance

---

[1] Bruce Orwall, *Wall Street Journal*, November 23, 2004.

package is strong evidence of his negotiating abilities, he completely failed to mitigate the organization, role, or personal risks.

Organization Risk

The main organization risks are the lack of a winning strategy or the organization's inability to implement that strategy. You are trying to make sure you do not go into an organization that is doomed to failure no matter what you do.

When doing your due diligence on organizational risk, be sure to assess risk elements in the areas that we call the Five Cs: Customers, Collaborators, Capabilities, Competitors, and Conditions. The good news is that you probably have a significant head start on understanding many of these or you wouldn't be being considered for the job. But do not rely on what you think you know. Go through the exercise and see what new things you can learn. In particular, you need to understand all of these in relation to the specific job you've been offered.

Five Cs

Customers: First line, customer chain, end users, influencers

Collaborators: Suppliers, allies, government/community leaders

Capabilities: Human, operational, financial, technical, key assets

Competitors: Direct, indirect, potential

Conditions: Social/demographic, political/government/regulatory, economic, market

To work through the Five Cs, talk to customers, suppliers, allies, employees (including your new direct reports), past employees, social—demographic—political—governmental—regulatory—economic experts, analysts, and journalists who cover the company. The goal is to understand one fundamental question:

What is the organization's sustainable competitive advantage?

Customers have a couple of subsets that are important to look at. These include the people your business sells to—direct customers who actually give you money. In many cases, those customers will have customers, and their customers will have customers, and so on down the line. Eventually, there are end-users or consumers of whatever the output of that chain is. Finally, there are a whole set of people who influence your various customers' purchase decisions. A customer analysis should take all of these into account.

One of the classic examples of an insight that came out of a thorough evaluation of a customer chain was done by Federal Express. They sold overnight delivery services to corporate purchasing departments who then enabled business managers to send things overnight. But it turned out the real decision makers were those managers' administrative assistants. So Federal Express targeted its marketing efforts not at the people who wrote the checks, but at the core influencers. They did this by aiming the advertising and media at those influencers and by having their drivers pick the packages up from the administrative assistants personally instead of going through an impersonal mailroom.

Collaborators include your suppliers, business allies, and people delivering complementary products and services. What links all these groups is that they will do better if you do better so it is in their best interest, whether they know it or not, to help you succeed. Think Microsoft and Intel. Think hotdogs and mustard.

Capabilities are what you have or do not have that can help you deliver a differentiated, better product or service to your customers. These include everything from access to materials and capital to plants and equipment to people to patents.

Competitors include anyone who your customers could give their money or attention to instead of you. Without completely restating everything everyone has ever said about marketing myopia, it is important to take a very wide view of potential competitors. Just as the railroad's real competitors are other forms of transportation like automobiles and airplanes, Coca-Cola's main competitors in England turn out to be ice cream and chocolate. Consumers choose between saving for their children's college education and taking them on a Disney World vacation. In analyzing these competitors, it is important to think through the consumer's objectives and strategies as well as strengths and weaknesses to give you the best possible chance to predict what they will really do.

Conditions are a catchall for everything going on in the environment in which you do business. It is important to look at social, political, demographic, and economic trends at a minimum.

Pulling It All Together

You want to pull all of this together in some sort of organizing framework. (By now you've figured out that we are strong supporters of organizing frameworks.) One good, basic tool is a strengths, weaknesses, opportunities, and threats analysis (SWOT). Use this tool to prompt your thinking about the sources, drivers, and hinderers of revenue and value and also insights and scenarios for the future. You will want to look at whether the current strategy and resource deployment is coherent and adequate. Look at the stated strategy and look hard at what the organization is really doing— the de facto strategy.

SWOT

A SWOT analysis is one of the best ways to get an accurate look at your team's or organization's current reality. Remember that strengths and weaknesses are internal, and opportunities and threats are external (see Tool 3.2 on p. 46).

Key leverage points are the internal strengths that can be brought to bear to take advantage of external opportunities. These are the corridors of ways to win. For example, if you have a strong beverage distribution system and the public water supply is contaminated, you could leverage your system to deliver safe bottled water to people.

Business issues are the areas of internal weakness that are particularly vulnerable to external threats. Fixing these are ways to avoid losing. For example, if you have only marginally acceptable safety standards in your plants and there is pending legislation to increase legal safety standards well beyond those that you currently meet, that is a potential issue or threat.

Finally, the sustainable competitive advantage is most likely one of the key leverage points that can be sustained in the face of business issues.

Lack of Strategy

Larry had joined an organization that did not have a strategy and had a weak team.[2] He'd taken a job as president of a division with no real competitive advantages, let alone ones that could be sustained over time. A major client in a different division that had left just before Larry joined had sustained the business. For whatever reason, Larry did not figure this out until he had been there a month. At that point, his options were to leave or work as hard as he could to survive. These were landmines he should have seen well before he started by uncovering them during due diligence.

Lack of Competitive Advantage

Louisa had been looking for a job for 18 months. She took a job with a growing division of a major player in the software business. They were trying to expand into a completely new area and asked her to come in as vice president of marketing for the new group. She had been lobbying for the general manager job, but settled for the marketing job because she was so excited about the new division's prospects. She should not have been.

As it turned out, the division had no competitive advantage and was competing against an entrenched competitor that had quickly stepped into the gap that Louisa's new company had staked the division's future on. Six months into the job, Louisa recommended the company abandon the effort and focus its efforts on other things. Right recommendation. Bad for Louisa. She was out of a job again.

Role Risk

Role risk has a couple of components. There is a role risk when the expectations and resources are not aligned. There is also a role risk when stakeholders do not agree on what those expectations and resources are. You need to understand a couple of things about the role to complete your due diligence:

---

[2] The stories in this book are real. We've changed the names, places, and industries to preserve confidentiality as appropriate. So don't get hung up on the specifics. Look for the learning points.

- Why does the position exist? Why did they need to create it in the first place?
- Objectives/outcomes: What are you supposed to get done?
- What will the impact be on the rest of the organization? What kind of interactions can you expect with them.
- What are your specific responsibilities including your decision-making authority and people reporting to you.

The fundamental issue here has to do with making sure the key stakeholders are aligned around the role's reason to exist, objectives, impact, and responsibilities. It is almost guaranteed that these were not always aligned. You need to find out whether they have actually ever been aligned. Your work here is geared to answering the question:

Who had concerns about the way the role was designed; and what was done to make them feel better about it now?

There are a couple of parts to this:

1. Finding the people who had concerns
2. Understanding those concerns
3. Understanding what has changed to make those concerns go away
4. Believing that those people will support the role (and you) going forward

Reporting Lines

One new president had done a great job of negotiating his title and package, but had failed to consider things like reporting lines and resources. He soon learned that neither the head of marketing, CFO, CIO, nor HR manager reported to him. His only direct reports were the heads of sales and business development. By taking the title of president, without the appropriate authority, all he had managed to do was to paint a target on his back for his peers to shoot at so they could get him out of the way and strengthen their own positions.

Understanding the role is important. But what about understanding the company?

Elwanda was thrilled! They had recruited her out of the country's second largest supermarket chain and offered her the job of brand manager of Coca-Cola, the #1 brand in the country, and she was going to be in charge!

Her first few days on the job were wonderful. Everyone was so nice and so professional. It was clearly a well-run organization. She met the promotional team, the vending team, the trade marketing team, the legal team, the sales team, even the key manufacturing and distribution people.

After she had met most of the key people in the company, she went into the city to meet the advertising agency. This was less wonderful. Not only was the agency not that interested in her point of view on the advertising, it turned out she did not actually work for The Coca-Cola Company. She worked for their local bottler/distributor.

In her country, like most countries around the world, The Coca-Cola Company sold ingredients to bottlers who bottled and distributed product to retail outlets. The Coca-Cola Company kept responsibility for all product formulation, package design, consumer promotion, and advertising. The bottler was responsible for manufacturing, pricing, sales, and distribution.

So, while Elwanda had thought she was going to be in charge of all the marketing of the Coca-Cola brand, in fact, she was limited to creating and developing in-store point-of-purchase materials—subject to the approval of The Coca-Cola Company's local brand team. The bottler had created a whole, separate, redundant organization. And she didn't figure it out until a week into the job.

Core Team

Rod was looking at a role as executive vice president (EVP) of sales. One of the things that attracted him was the CEO telling him that the EVP of sales was part of his core team. If this was true, why did the role report to the COO who in turn reported to the CEO? Rod dug into it, figured out that the role was not really part of the core team, and turned down the job.

CEO or Peace Maker?

Samantha was brought from a large supermarket chain as head of distribution into a new role for a major publishing company as COO. After years of hearing from investors and the board that he should professionalize management of what had grown into a large business out of a single flagship publication, the CEO changed his own title (he had been the publisher) and hired Samantha. It took three months for Samantha to learn what some up-front investigative work could have told her: The CEO actually did not make executive decisions. Ever. Everything was a negotiated truce between factions that were constantly at war, and he ran the company the way Congress runs its budget—pork barrel politics. There was no strategy and no operations to speak of and her own job was just such an accommodation with the board. There was only one way to go: out.

Strategy or Operations?

Helena was hired to replace an outgoing managing director for Le Monde Interactif, the web version of the newspaper. She had a strong background in consulting for media companies, with expertise in Internet marketing. The CEO of the parent company, nervous about a world he did not quite understand, felt comforted by having her expertise on board. In the first few weeks, the senior managers reviewed strategy and appreciated her input. Soon, however, the focus turned to classic management and operational concerns. Helena had very little experience with these and found her portfolio of responsibilities shifting and shrinking. In the end, an accommodation was made and she handled negotiating contracts with service providers. But this was a far cry from what she had thought she had been brought in to do, and she regretted not having asked enough questions from enough people up front.

Personal Risk

Personal risk occurs when you oversell yourself. There is nothing wrong with overselling yourself to others. Just make sure you take a hard look at the reality before you jump into the wrong situation. The basic questions are:

- Is this the company and role that can best capitalize on your strengths over time?
- Will you look forward to coming to work three years from now?
- Will you fit in with the culture?

A good way to get at some of these is to ask:

What, specifically, about me, led to you offering me the job?

The goal is to find out what they saw as your strengths, motivation, fit, and compare them to your own reality. If there are significant differences, don't be afraid to address them directly, and think about walking away.

Requisite Skills

A Wall Street brokerage firm needed a division manager. They considered one of their existing employees. Xavier was a highly analytical, numbers-focused employee who also had a strong suit in technology development. He had actually written well over half the code the firm used in his division. And he was remarkably good at his core job as well—as a sell-side analyst. Even better, from the point of view of senior management, he didn't make waves, didn't have ambitions to take over the company, and would accept less pay and create fewer problems than someone from outside this very insular company. It was easy to offer him the promotion. And why would he say no to such an opportunity?

Two years later when the firm finally hired a "star" manager who had the requisite skills—management experience, leadership, charisma, and yes, ambition to help motivate the very ambitious troops—the truth of Xavier's mistake became apparent. No longer a rising star, he had to settle back down among the troops, this time tarnished with a failure.

Fit with the Way Things Are Done around Here

Sam had grown up in small advertising and public relations agencies. He took a job with a Fortune 100 company as director of publicity. We met with Sam on his first day in the new job. One of his questions was "How do I handle all the e-mails? I'm already getting 15 a day and it's overwhelming." Some of you reading this are thinking 15 is nothing. But to Sam it was a lot. The underlying issue was that Sam had no experience navigating the systems and politics of a large corporation from the inside. Sam was used to small groups that actually talked to each other. (Not necessarily a bad thing, by the way.) Sam found large company processes overwhelming and had to leave relatively quickly. Ideally, Sam should have figured this out before accepting the role.

Fundamental Questions

Everyone has his or her own way of doing due diligence. However you do it, you *must* feel good about the answers to these three questions before accepting a job:

1. What is the organization's sustainable competitive advantage?
2. Who had concerns about the way the role was designed and what was done to make them feel better about it now?
3. What, specifically, about me, led to you offering me the job?

HOT TIP

Due Diligence Questions: Do not accept a job until you've answered these fundamental questions. It is far less painful to turn down the wrong job than it is to suffer the agony of dealing with organizational, role, and personal landmines later.

Making It Happen

In many ways, the first data you will get regarding your due diligence is how open the company is to you doing it. If the company is open to you learning everything you can before you accept, that is a very good sign. If the company absolutely blocks you from learning anything, be careful.

You should start by laying out your due diligence plan with the person who offered you the job. Let him know what you want to learn and how you want to do it. Position this along the lines that you want to learn as much as you can before you accept because you're anticipating this being a very long-term relationship and you want to make absolutely sure the fit is right.

You will want information from people who can give you perspective on each of the Five Cs. So talk to:

Customers and people that call on customers

Collaborators including suppliers, agencies, and people who deal with them

People who can help you understand the organization's *capabilities* including your future direct reports, peers, outside analysts, people who left the company, and the like

Competitors and people who understand competitors, including many of the people who understand the organization's capabilities

People who understand how changing external *conditions* may impact the organization including outside analysts and many of the people mentioned in this list

In each case, communicate your excitement and interest in the company and probe for real understanding.

Due diligence is hard work. But doing it is nowhere near as painful as discovering things later that you wish you'd known ahead of time—like which company you're really joining. To be fair, very few people do a complete due diligence before accepting a new job. But later, many wish they had.

Due Diligence—Summary and Implications

The second step in successful on-boarding, doing your due diligence, occurs between offer and acceptance. During this step, you should be making sure the job is right for you, mitigating organization, role, and personal risks by answering three questions:

1. What is the organization's sustainable competitive advantage?
2. Who had concerns about the way the role was designed and what was done to make them feel better about it now?
3. What, specifically, about me, led to you offering me the job?

Having worked as hard as you did to get offered the new role; it's going to be painful and perhaps embarrassing to turn it down. But, if it's wrong for you or you're wrong for it, that's exactly what you're going to have to do.

QUESTIONS YOU SHOULD ASK YOURSELF

- Is this the right organization and role for me?
- Am I the right person for this organization and role at this point in my career?

Downloadable TOOL 3.1
Five Cs Situation Analysis Guidelines*

1. Customers (first line, customer chain, end users, influencers)

Needs, hopes, preference, commitment, strategies, price/value perspective by segment

First line/direct customers:

- Universe of opportunity—Total market, volume by segment
- Current situation—Volume by customer; profit by customer

Customer chain:

- Customers' customers—Total market, volume by segment
- Current customers' strategies, volume, and profitability by segment

End users:

- Preference, consumption, usage, loyalty, and price value data and perceptions for products and competitors' products

Influencers:

- Key influencers of customer and end-user purchase and usage decisions

2. Collaborators (suppliers, business allies, complementors, government/community leaders)

- Strategies, profit/value models for external and internal stakeholders (up, across, down)

3. Capabilities

- Human (includes style and quality of management, strategy dissemination, culture: values, norms, focus, discipline, innovation, teamwork, execution, urgency, politics)
- Operational (includes integrity of business processes, effectiveness of organization structure, links between measures and rewards and corporate governance)
- Financial (includes capital and asset utilization and investor management)

Downloadable TOOL 3.1   (Continued)

- Technical (includes core processes, IT systems, supporting skills)
- Key assets (includes brands and intellectual property)

4. Competitors (direct, indirect, potential)

- Strategies, profit/value models, profit pools by segment, source of pride

5. Conditions

- Social/demographic—trends
- Political/government/regulatory—trends
- Economic—macro and micro—trends
- Market definition, inflows, outflows, substitutes, and so on—trends

Pulling It Together

SWOT analysis and thinking about:

- Sources, drivers, hinderers of revenue and value
- Insights and scenarios (to set up: *What/So What/Now What?*)
- Current strategy/resource deployment: Coherent? Adequate? De facto strategy?

Downloadable TOOL 3.2
SWOT Form*

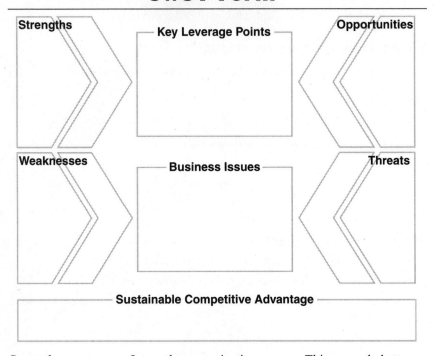

Strengths:	Internal to organization	Things we do better
Weaknesses:	Internal to organization	Things we do worse
Opportunities:	External to organization	Things to capitalize on
Threats:	External to organization	Things to worry about

Key leverage points: Opportunities we can leverage our strengths against (where play to win)

Business implications: Threats our weaknesses make us vulnerable to (where play not to lose)

Sustainable competitive advantages: Key leverage points that can be sustained over an extended period of time

---

Downloadable TOOL 3.3
Due Diligence Checklist*

Key questions to answer during due diligence:

1. Mitigate organizational risk.

What is the organization's sustainable competitive advantage?

_____

_____

_____

_____

_____

2. Mitigate role risk.

Who had concerns about the way the role was designed and what was done
to make them feel better about it now?

_____

_____

_____

_____

_____

3. Mitigate personal risk.

What specifically about me led to you offering me the job?

_____

_____

_____

_____

_____

THE 100-DAY
ACTION PLAN

CHAPTER 4

You Must Start *before* Day One

ESPECIALLY WITH YOUR BOSS AND KEY STAKEHOLDERS

Part I—Before you accept a new leadership role: **SELL** yourself first; Do your **DUE DILIGENCE**

Part II—The New Leader's 100-Day Action Plan

Fuzzy Front End	DAY ONE	30	45	60	70	100

You must start BEFORE Day One

Take Control of DAY ONE

Use key MILESTONES to drive team performance

Get the right people in the right ROLES

Decide how to ENGAGE the new Culture

Get buy in for the one BURNING IMPERATIVE and create the new strategy

Invest in EARLY WINS to build team confidence

Shape the team CULTURE with an ongoing communication campaign

Part III—What leaders know:
ADJUST to inevitable surprises; **AVOID** the most common mistakes;
BUILD loyalty, trust, and commitment

WARNING!

If you have already started your new role, this chapter may upset you. It is full of ideas for people to implement *before* they start. The best way to take charge, build your team, and get great results—faster than anyone thought possible—is to cheat by creating time by starting earlier than anyone thought you would. That is what this chapter's about.

Even if you have already started, you still need to read this chapter because if you have not done the things laid out here, you need to do them, now—even if you are already in the role.

At first, Nathaniel did not buy the concept that he should start before his official Day One. He wanted to take some time off so that he could show up at his new job rested and relaxed. Further, he initially thought some of the ideas in this chapter were manipulative and not the way he wanted to act at all. We persuaded him to listen to what we had to say and eventually he agreed to try a few of our suggested actions before Day One. Here is what he wrote a week later:

> *I've already reached out to some future colleagues and some agency counterparts just to introduce myself. You're right, it is game-changing. Everyone has reacted with warmth and candor and it will make the first few weeks far more effective and enjoyable.*

Everything new leaders do and say and *don't* do and *don't* say sends powerful signals, starting well before they even walk in the door. One of the crucial mistakes that many leaders make is to fall into the trap of thinking that leadership begins on Day One of a new job. Like it or not, a new leader's role begins as soon as he or she is acknowledged as a candidate for the job.

The realization of that reality can either make or break a new leader's transition. By missing this key point, new leaders often discover, in hindsight, that organizational and/or market momentum was working against their successful transition even before they showed up for their first full day at the office. Those leaders that recognize that their jobs start well before Day One gain valuable "free" time to direct the flow of momentum, before they arrive. We refer to this bonus time as the fuzzy front end.[1]

The fuzzy front end often comes at the worst possible time, interfering with the last days of an old job, or with time earmarked for vacation, catching up with household errands, or generally unwinding a little before the big day. The good news is that, more often than not, key elements of the fuzzy front end can be addressed in relatively short order. Even so, strive to stretch out the fuzzy front end between acceptance and the start date; and skip or shorten that planned vacation. Establishing a fuzzy front end, by adding days before your official start, is quite possibly the best way to get more done during the first 100 days of a complex transition.

---

[1] The early stages of a new product development process are often referred to as the fuzzy front end. Since we're talking about on-boarding as a team development process, the term works well.

Everything communicates during the fuzzy front end and nothing says more during this phase than how the new leader sets his priorities. To enjoy the benefits of a successful fuzzy front end, it is essential to remember that new leaders set their priorities with their calendars. When things are done, and in what order, is crucial. Thus, it is important to get personally set up, gather information, listen, learn, and begin leading all at the same time. These elements are essential if you want to get a head start before Day One.

Furthermore, this is one of the very few opportunities you'll ever have to create extra time and "white space"[2] before jumping in. You can use this time for mental and physical preparation, and for prestart meetings and phone calls to jumpstart relationships and learning.

You may also use part of the time to be a "fly on the wall" and gather all sorts of intelligence with little or no recognition. Think of how often you would have liked to have been a fly on the wall during other parts of your career where you could quietly gather information and observations that would give you a special advantage going forward. The fuzzy front end is one of the few times in your career where you will have that luxury.

Key steps for the "fuzzy front end" include:

- Identify key stakeholders.
- Manage personal set up.
- Conduct prestart meetings and phone calls.
- Gather prestart information and learning.
- Plan your first 100 days.

Key Stakeholders

Step one is to identify the key stakeholders up, across, and down. Key stakeholders are those people who can directly impact your strategy and thus your career. Many transitioning executives fail to think through this process or look in only one direction to find their key stakeholders. Others make the mistake of treating everyone as a

---

[2] Malcolm Gladwell describes the difference white space can make between success and failure in *Blink*, New York: Little Brown, 2005.

key stakeholder and end up trying to please everybody. Clearly, both of these approaches are doomed to fail.

Key stakeholders are found in three directions: up, across, and down. Those three areas are in direct relationship to where you place yourself in the organization. Up includes your boss, your indirect boss if there is a matrix organization, your boss's boss, the board of directors, your boss's assistant, or anyone else that resides further up in the organization who can have a direct opinion of or impact on your success.

Across you'll find key stakeholders who might include key allies, peers, customers, clients, partners, or even the person who wanted your job but didn't get it. Down will usually include your direct reports and other critical support people who are essential to successful implementation of your team's goals.

Just figuring out who all these people are can be a task in itself. Fortunately, this is not something new executives have to do by themselves. Generally, there will be a human resource contact, a boss, or an internal mentor who can help identify these people. You can often identify key stakeholders by observing the person who previously held the role. If they were successful, they might provide some insight. If they were not successful, you can be sure that they probably missed or underserved a key stakeholder, so it is important to figure out who that was and why they were underserved. Some key stakeholders will be apparent, others will be hidden from view, so do not be afraid to ask when you are building your list.

While it is important to keep the key stakeholder list to a manageable size, we recommend that, in the beginning, if you are not sure whether or not someone is a key stakeholder, keep them on the list until you are certain they are not. Ignoring a key stakeholder can have a devastating impact on a new leader and might kill any chance of a successful transition. If you are unsure of where to place a key stakeholder, it's better to first place him above where you think he should be and move him down later rather than placing him lower than where he should actually be. That mistake is sometimes hard to recover from so avoid it at all costs. Also, keep in mind that key stakeholders are sometimes very elusive. So once this list is made, you should constantly monitor the situation to ensure that all the right people are included.

The other thing your internal contact can help you figure out is which of the stakeholders should form your internal board. These are people you are going to treat differently because of their influence or impact—regardless of their explicit roles in the hierarchy. You're going to treat them like board members—never surprise them in meetings and make sure they get the chance to give you informal, off-the record advice. Set the stage early and position yourself as an executive who is eager for and welcomes feedback from your internal board.

Candidates for your internal board are people who are going to have an undue influence on your boss or your ability to get things done. Think in terms of some of your key peers. Think in terms of people who have been with your boss for a long time. Think in terms of people who seem to enjoy the mentor role. Think in terms of people who are trusted advisors within the organization.

Once identified, develop individual relationships with your internal board members and plan to develop deep relationships with them. If you are in the position to do so, and it's appropriate, play the same role for them, when appropriate.

There Are Always Key Stakeholders in Addition to Your Boss

Kevin had been brought into the organization to make deep and substantial changes to the way the information systems worked. Kevin was charged with completely reinventing the information system structure so that it might more efficiently support the organization's growth objectives. It was hoped that Kevin's changes would, in turn, drive deep and substantial changes to the way the entire organization worked. Kevin walked into a complex situation and lost the battle early on by failing to recognize the key stakeholders other than his boss. In the end, Kevin got blown up by a couple of different landmines:

- His new *role* had never been agreed on by all the key stakeholders, so as a result Kevin experienced substantial turf battles from Day One. Had he properly identified them early on, he might have had a chance at developing consensus among the group and avoiding the turf battles that ensued.
- His *personal* way of working did not fit with the organization's base culture. Somewhere along the line, Kevin should have had

key stakeholders who could have helped him accurately identify the important elements of organizational culture. Kevin's
failing was that he never identified his Across stakeholders and
made the common mistake of assuming that peers were not key
stakeholders. (They were.)

- He was unable to *deliver* the results expected in the timing expected because he did not build a high-performing team fast
  enough. He never identified his Down stakeholders. He mistak-
  enly thought that there could not be any stakeholders hiding
  out in the Down area of the organization. As a result, he was
  unable to get buy-in on his plans.

- He was unable to *adjust* when his boss was replaced. Once his
  only identified key stakeholder left, he had no one else in the
  Up area to look out for him or his initiatives.

Kevin chose to enter this organization, with all its landmines,
like a bull in a china shop. He was there to make changes and he expected those that did not like them to get out of his way. It ended
early for Kevin because he missed the importance of recognizing his
key stakeholders. In fact, he never paused to build personal relationships with any of his key stakeholders beyond his immediate boss.
When his boss was moved on, Kevin had no other allies Up, Across,
or Down. Building relationships with key stakeholders early on
would have provided Kevin a much better chance of surviving the
many risks of his transition. Without them, he had no chance at all.

Your Most Important Stakeholder Is Your Boss
(In Fact or in His View)

Frank was moving from one country to a major role in another
country. In the new country, he was going to have a dual responsibility for (1) a brand's strategies worldwide and (2) that brand's
business in the new country. He told us he reported to the worldwide head of marketing on the brand's strategies and had a *peer* relationship with the country's general manager.

It sounded good.

But, a week before Frank was to start in his new role, we discovered that the country general manager thought Frank reported to him.

"Frank, what gives?"

"He's a peer."

"But he thinks he's your boss."

"He's a peer."

"You may be right. But he thinks he's your boss. And you probably don't want to walk in Day One treating him like a peer."

If you are going to confuse where stakeholders fit, have a bias to upgrade them. You are not going to get in much trouble treating an Across like an Up or a Down like an Across. The opposite is not true.

Personal Set Up

The perfect office that is fully stocked and completely set up to your liking does not just suddenly appear. If you are lucky, you will have a place to call your own on your first day, but most likely, it will not be tailored to fit your needs or your style. Executives in new roles often underestimate the time, planning, and thinking required to get their office space right for what they need. Most executives make one of two mistakes when it comes to setting up their space. One mistake is to focus energy and attention in the first week on getting their office just right. What kind of message does that send? The other mistake is to work in a less than suitable environment for months while trying to find the time to get the office right. More often than not, that "time" never comes and as a result their performance may be hampered. Neither choice is good. The alternative solution is to get this critical, yet important, job done during the fuzzy front end.

You will need a place to work. This will involve, at a minimum, some sort of desk and chair. But think beyond that. Do you want an office? Do you want your predecessor's office? Do you want that office to have chairs, tables, couches? Think through how you like to work and what messages you want your workspace to communicate. Should it say "I'm the boss. I am powerful. Enter at your own risk." Or should it say "Come on in, sit down, and tell me what's on your mind?" Big desks say the former. Couches, say the latter.

There is no right answer to any of this. But part of preparing to lead is thinking through how you want to lead and the messages you want to send. And your physical workspace says a lot about you—even before people meet you.

Other physical things to consider about your workspace include: cabinets, white boards, flip charts, and the like. You'll need to think about what sort of technology you want to use to help you lead. This might include personal computer/laptop (with e-mail access), phones, cell phones, Blackberry, stationary, files, business cards, and so on. The checklist (Tool 4.5 on p. 76), once completed, will make it easier for you or an assistant to get the job done for you before Day One.

Get Your Space Right

Gerry had left one company and worked at the second company for six weeks. In an odd turn of events, the first company exercised the noncompete clause it had with Gerry that required him to re-sign from his new job and wait it out for 12 months. Luckily for Gerry, the second company wanted to hire him back after his non-compete expired.

We met Gerry a few weeks before he was about to reenter the sec-ond company and took him through the PrimeGenesis on-boarding, or in his case, reboarding preparation. When we got to the point about personal set-up, Gerry excitedly interrupted us.

"That's it!"

"That's what?"

"That's why I was so uncomfortable. I'd worked at my previous company for 23 years and never really thought about my office. Then I got here and felt uncomfortable. I always thought it was just the newness. But it's because I've always had a white board in my of-fice. I think on a white board. My office here didn't have one."

The HR person sitting in promised to make sure there was a white board in Gerry's office before he got there, so Gerry could "think."

As long as we are on the subject of personal set-up, it is worth-while to make sure someone is getting you access to the things that you will need. In today's technology-dominant, security-driven world, there are many things that are essential, yet, we often forget their importance. Without these things, it is often impossible to get work done. Think about items such as identification cards, garage or elevator passes, computers, network access, voice mail, e-mail ad-dress, and any number of passwords. It is best if all of these things are taken care of in the fuzzy front end.

Also, it is worthwhile to identify who can help you get set up. Usually it is helpful if someone other than yourself notifies the key support staff that you will be requiring their assistance before Day One. If you have not already negotiated this up front, it is important to know whether you will have an assistant. Do you want an assistant? What should be his skill set? Will you be sharing him with someone else? What is his current workload? Will you have an assigned mentor or HR representative to help you navigate the existing culture in the early days?

One of our most enlightened clients requires new senior leaders to come into the office two to three weeks before they start so they can physically see their space and pick color schemes, furniture layout, and the like. Now that is an organization that truly embraces the fuzzy front end!

Family

Just as you have people following you in the business world, you may have personal followers. No matter how much you try, you are not going to be able to give the business your best efforts until you have your family comfortable. Taking the time to figure out housing, schools, transportation, and the like is not a luxury. It is a business imperative. And there is no better time to get this resolved than during the fuzzy front end or before.

The main point about personal set up—both in the office and home—is that this is something you can get in motion well before you actually show up for work. There are going to be enough other things to worry about in the early days of a complex transition that you do not want to be rummaging around for a computer, door key, or school for your children. Get those things set well in advance.

Prestart Meetings and Phone Calls

As we have said, everything you do communicates. This includes who you talk to, in what forum, and in what order. People will view the order in which you talk to people as a sign of their relative importance. Starting Day One, that order is indelible. The people you talk to early will feel valued. The people you talk to later will feel slighted.

There is a physical limitation to how many people you can talk to on Day One or week one and so on. The good news about the fuzzy front end is that it allows you to create time by starting before Day One. If the people you talk to on Day One feel valued, the people you talk to *before* Day One feel even more valued. And the answers you get to questions before you actually start will be different from the answers you get after you start. You are a different person before you start. You are not yet an employee or boss. You are just someone looking to make a connection and learn.

You should have meetings with the "most important" stakeholders Up, Across, and Down if at all practical and phone calls with the other important stakeholders. The most important stakeholders are the ones who are going to be most critical to your surviving and thriving in the new role. These might include:

- Your new boss
- The most influential board members
- Critical peers—especially ones who were candidates for your new job
- Critical customers and clients
- Critical direct reports—especially ones who were candidates for your new job or are considered to be flight risks

These early conversations can make a huge difference. One executive was coming into a company as the corporate chief marketing officer. His critical peers included six division presidents. A week before he started he had still not met three of them. We pointed out that the impression he was going to make on them and the support he was going to get from them was going to be hugely different if he met them for the first time in week two than if he met them before he started. He got on a plane and met each of them face-to-face that week. His colleagues were overwhelmed by his willingness to start a relationship with them before his official Day One and they appreciated the chance to get to know him on a more personal basis before he started. As a result, when the official start date rolled around, our client already had relationships established with most of his key stakeholders. He was astounded at the headstart these introductions gave him in implementing his plan.

The impact you can make by reaching out to one of these critical stakeholders before they start is incalculable. Yet, we are surprised at how reluctant some executives are to set up those meetings. They often expect to encounter resistance, but rarely do. To make the process easier, here are some suggestions for how you might start the conversation:

"Hi Jack, I'm Jill. I'll be starting in two weeks as president. Stuart has told me that you're an absolutely critical part of the team. I didn't want to show up without getting a chance to meet you in advance."

"Bob, since you're such a valued customer of my new company; I can't imagine starting work without getting to know you first. I'll meet you anywhere in the world that's most convenient for you, anytime that's most convenient for you over the next month. I'd really love to have your perspective on what's going on before I start."

"Andrew, since you weren't on the board's search committee, we haven't met. But I'd love to spend some time with you before I start. . . ."

Immediate Impact of a Prestart Conversation

Bill was joining a company as senior vice president of sales. The previous senior vice president of sales had switched over to head up client relations with the firm's largest customers. We were brought in to help Bill with his on-boarding, but not until the Friday before he started. We talked to him between his son's Little League baseball games on Saturday and identified the previous head of sales as someone he should reach out to if possible. He agreed, and he had what he thought was a nice, but not particularly important conversation with the former head of sales on Sunday.

Then, on his first official day the following Monday, Bill talked to each of his direct reports one-on-one. Each and every one of them mentioned that they had talked to the previous head of sales who had told them that he thought Bill was a "good guy" who would be an asset. Wow! One carefully selected conversation gained Bill the luxury of walking in the door on Day One with instant credibility and support.

Missing Big Groups

Stuart was joining a large bank to head up its Asian operations. He had met most of the key corporate headquarters stakeholders in Zurich before he accepted the job. We were talking to him about stakeholders and digging into which product lines he was going to be responsible for. It turned out the bank had just bought another, smaller bank located in Germany. Not surprisingly, Stuart had never met anyone at the acquired bank.

At our suggestion, he got on a plane and spent two days at the acquired bank getting to know its key players before he actually started his job. He made a huge impact on the people he met who were extraordinarily impressed that he came to visit them on his own time. Even if they were concerned about other people at the headquarters, they knew they were on Stuart's radar screen at least—getting those relationships off to a great start.

Tackling Risk on Your Own Timetable

Sometimes it is appropriate to combine these meetings with a little due diligence. Ben had been offered a job as chief marketing officer of a fast-growing Internet company. After being offered the position, he asked if he could meet some members of the board since they were playing an active role in the company.

"What if they don't like you? We've already made you an offer."

"If they don't like me, I want to know before I accept. I'd rather have you withdraw the offer than fire me later. Plus, by letting them weigh in now, they'll have some ownership over my entry. This will help me down the road."

So Ben met them. They did not withdraw the offer and things went well. By doing this, Ben eliminated one potential risk and sent a strong message to the board that he thought their buy-in was important.

Getting Rid of Problems Ahead of Time

Elliot was about to join a small company as vice president of marketing. The search had originally been for a director of marketing. The CEO had met and hired two people he liked at that level before he met Elliot. He was so impressed with Elliot, he hired him to come in on top of the two people he had just hired.

The two directors had not started yet.

At our suggestion, Elliot had them fly over and meet him before he started.

This turned out to be a good idea because Elliot was not impressed with either one. He went back to the CEO and probed why they were hired. It came out that the CEO really had not been all that impressed with them either. But, since he hadn't met Elliot, he thought they were the best available. Elliot was able to convince the CEO to withdraw their offers, avoiding two problems even before he (or they) started.

HOT TIP

Meet with Critical Stakeholders before You Start: This one idea is worth many times whatever you paid for this book. Contacting key stakeholders before you start always makes a huge difference. It is a game changer.

Just asking for the premeeting makes an impact. Coming in with an open mind and really listening to what people have to say is fundamental. We have found that structuring the conversations is important as well. We suggest breaking the conversations into learning, expectations, and implementation. Even before that though, your first question is probably something along the lines of "tell me about yourself." You want to understand your key stakeholders as people. You want to understand their personal wants and needs as well as their business issues. Once you understand that, you can move on to learning, expectations, and implementation:

- *Learning:* During the learning part of your conversations, you should focus on two key areas: perceptions and strengths. Perceptions have to do with understanding each stakeholder's assessment of the situation at hand. A good way to gather perceptions is to ask how she thinks things are going in general and then use questions from the five Cs analysis to get at more specifics. Both are useful ways to identify individual's perceptions on key issues.

    Different stakeholders will have different views of the same situation. Some will think things are going well. Some will look at upside opportunities for the future. And some will tell you things are not going well and need to be turned around quickly to prevent an impending disaster. During this learning phase, keep in mind that getting at the truth is less important than understanding the key stakeholders' perceptions of the situation. Those perceptions will indicate how you might best interact with that key stakeholder in relation to the situation being evaluated.

Once you've learned a stakeholder's view of the situation, you also want to get his input in terms of the five Cs that we described earlier: Customers, Collaborators, Capabilities, Competitors, and Conditions. Use each of these Cs as a guideline for your discussion.

The second part of the learning phase is the identification of strengths. It is useful to understand the different stakeholders' perceptions of what strengths exist in the organization and what strengths need to be developed in order for the organization to be even more successful.

- *Expectations:* You will want to understand what their view is of the priorities (and untouchables) of the situation, and what resources are required and available. These conversations will be different Up, Across, and Down. Up you're looking for direction. Across you're looking to build mutual understanding. Down you're looking for current reality and needs. While your questions will be different for each group, with all you will want to know what their priorities are and what they think your priorities should be.

  Throughout this process, your objective should be to seek information first in order to understand. Ask questions, listen well, and don't offer your opinion yet. At this point, you just don't know enough to offer an opinion and most likely you cannot provide any reasonable direction to anybody. So don't try. Take the pressure off yourself and just ask and listen using the above frameworks.

- *Implementation:* Here you're looking to understand (1) how people communicate; (2) how decisions are to be made in terms of who makes them; and (3) what things are really measured, tracked, and how—the control points.

Communication

Most of us realize the importance of communication. There are three areas of communication that you will need to understand about each stakeholder regardless of where they are located. If you understand a stakeholder's communication preferences—mode, manner, and frequency—you will significantly reduce the risk of any communication snafus. Still, many executives do not know how to decipher the best ways to communicate to key stakeholders. We have an excellent solution: If they are an Up or an Across stakeholder, ask them. If they are a Down stakeholder, tell them:

- *Mode:* This is simple. How does the stakeholder prefer to receive information? Different people have different preferences. Is it e-mail, voicemail, in-person, memos, or something else? Sending voicemails to e-mail people is as unproductive as sending e-mails to voicemail people. Communication is useless unless and until it has been received.

  Charlie had two bosses. Neither used computers. One prided himself on never reading his mail, but he checked his voicemails regularly. The other boss was so afraid of the phone that he had his secretary type out his voicemail messages, but he read his mail regularly. So Charlie would write the second boss a note and then dictate it into the first boss's voicemail.

- *Manner:* Just understanding mode is not enough. You need to understand manner as well. Manner is similar to social behavior or style. In what way or style does the stakeholder like to receive his information? Two people might say they prefer face-to-face meetings. One might want you to stop by anytime, put your feet on the desk, and share early ideas. The other might want you to make an appointment with her secretary at least two weeks in advance and make sure all the key players have provided input into your PowerPoint deck before you share it with her. Both of these are face-to-face meetings (mode), but their manners are very different.

- *Frequency:* This answers the question of how often. Different management styles demand different frequencies of communication. Shame on you if you wander in for your monthly update with your boss and she says, "Where have you been? I expected weekly updates." Shame on you if you come in for your third weekly update and your boss says "Why are you here every week? You are a senior player. I hired you to run your operations. Come to me if there's a problem or update me monthly." Like the other elements of communication, frequency preferences will vary greatly so, ask in advance.

Decisions

Without question, all stakeholders will have a different way of making decisions. Decisions can be made in a variety of ways and it's crucial that a new executive understand how the key stakeholders like to and expect to make decisions. Again, it comes down to the simple solution of asking.

A helpful scale for understanding how decisions between person A and person B can be made is shown in Tool 4.3 on page 72.

In general, you want to push things to levels 2 and 4 (either person A or B makes decision with input from the other). Input is helpful whether its approval, consultation, or information. And shared decisions have a nasty tendency not to be made by anyone.

Control Points

Different organizations use different metrics and processes for controlling what is really going on. You need to know what they are. What are the key measures of success along the way? How are they tracked? Meetings? Reports?

Prestart Information and Learning

There is a whole set of information you can get and go through before you meet anyone in the new organization. These include things people have written down in terms of: key documents, financials, customers, competitors, collaborators, current capabilities, market information, business environment, macro trends, share, distribution, pricing, merchandising, advertising, promotion, packaging, product, presence, public relations, operations, key contacts.

You can get these and go through them before you show up for your first day of work in your new role. They will help you start to put things in context and help you figure out what you want to do on that first day, during that first week, and during those first 100 days.

Learning

Some learning will have taken place during due diligence. Some will take place before you show up. Some will take place after you start the job. There is a lot to learn and the five Cs list is not designed to be all inclusive. Instead, think of it as a starting point. Think back on the "fly on the wall" point. This is a great time to do an in-depth dive into your new organization's products and services.

For example, one consumer marketer for a restaurant chain started by spending six weeks in the restaurants working every job. He set up a chat room for the full six weeks to communicate with his team about what he was noticing about customers. This had a couple of goals:

1. Learn about the organization's products and services from the inside.
2. Communicate his bias of "customers first" to his team by his being in the restaurants.
3. Further communicate "customers first" by gearing his chat to customer issues.
4. Learning how his team thought by their reactions and input to his chat initiatives.

It is not important to have learned everything before you show up, but it is crucial to have a plan to learn in place. Your learning plan, like all plans, will evolve as you get more knowledgeable. Nevertheless, having that starting plan in place in advance will make everything else easier.

Fuzzy Front End—Summary and Implications

Key steps for the "fuzzy front end" include:

- Identify key stakeholders Up, Across, and Down.
- Manage personal set-up.
- Conduct prestart meetings and phone calls.
- Gather prestart information and learning.
- Plan your first 100 days.

The prestart meetings and phone calls are a great chance to jumpstart relationships by getting at learning, expectations, and implementation. We can't make this any clearer. You should do this. The benefits are huge.

QUESTIONS YOU SHOULD ASK YOURSELF

- Do I have the time I need before I start? (And if not, can I create it?)
- Have I optimized the time I've got?

Downloadable TOOL 4.1
100-Day Checklist*

Stakeholders

Up:

_____

_____

Across:

_____

_____

Down:

_____

_____

Fuzzy Front End

Personal set-up:

_____

_____

Meet live:

_____

_____

Phone calls:

_____

_____

Info/documents:

_____

_____

(continued)

Day One

_____

_____

First Week(s)

_____

_____

Tactical Capacity Building Blocks: **How**

Burning imperative in place (by day 30): _____

Milestones set (by day 45): _____

Strategies/Plans set for early wins (by day 60): _____

Team roles assessed and aligned (by day 70): _____

Team culture/communication steps: _____

Downloadable TOOL 4.2
Stakeholder List*

	Name	Position	Interaction Plan

Up (management)

_____

_____

_____

Key peers, internal allies, customers, and suppliers

_____

_____

_____

External customers and suppliers

_____

_____

_____

Direct/indirect reports

_____

_____

_____

Others

_____

_____

_____

Downloadable TOOL 4.3
On-Boarding
Conversation Framework*

Key questions to ask during on-boarding conversations (in addition to all the questions you would normally ask).

Learning

• Give me your read on the general *situation?*

_____

_____

• What *strengths/capabilities* are required for the task at hand?

_____

_____

• Which exist now?

_____

_____

Expectations

• What do you see as key *priorities?* Lower priorities? Current untouchables?

_____

_____

• What *resources* are available to invest against these priorities?

_____

_____

Implementation

• Tell me about the *control points.* (metrics and process: meetings, reports)

_____

_____

(continued)

Downloadable TOOL 4.3　(Continued)

- Tell me about some of the key *decisions* we make.

  Who makes them? How?

1	2	3	4	5
A on own	A with B's input	A&B share	B with A's input	B on own

- What's the best way to *communicate* with you?

  (Mode? Manner? Frequency?)

_____

_____

_____

_____

Downloadable TOOL 4.4
Relocation Checklist*

ASAP

- Get set up: Create move file, post calendar, and so on.

- Choose a moving company. Get multiple bids and references.

- Research schools at destination. Public? Independent?

- Start to gather children's essential records in a secure folder that travels with you.

- Choose a real estate agent at destination.

- Make arrangements to sell or rent your current home.

- Make travel arrangements for family and pets.

- Research temporary housing options in case they become necessary.

- Look hard at your possessions for things to give away or sell.

- Start a log of moving expenses for employer or taxes.

- Start to gather information about resources in destination city.

One Month before Moving Day

- Fill out change of address forms (for IRS, subscriptions and bills, etc.).

- Obtain medical and dental records, x-rays and prescription histories.

- Set up a checking account and safe deposit box in your new city.

- Take inventory of your belongings before they are packed, ideally with pictures.

- Arrange for help on moving day, especially looking after children.

Two Weeks before Moving Day

- Confirm travel reservations.

- Clean rugs and clothing and have them wrapped for moving.

- Close bank accounts and have your funds wired to your new bank.

---

* Copyright © PrimeGenesis® LLC. To customize this document, download Tool 4.4 to your hard drive from www.primegenesis.com/tools.html. The document can then be opened, edited, and printed using Microsoft Word or another popular word processing application.

Downloadable TOOL 4.4   (Continued)

- Check with your insurance agent to ensure you will be covered through your homeowner's or renter's policy during the move.

- Give a close friend or relative your travel route and schedule.

One Week before Moving Day

- Switch utility services to new address.

- Prearrange for important services—such as a working phone.

- Collect valuables (important documents, jewelry, etc.) from safe-deposit boxes, or other depositories.

On Move-Out Day

- Be sure valuables are secure and ready to go with you. Carry important documents, currency, and jewelry yourself, or use registered mail.

- If customary, have cash to tip movers.

- Have water, drinks, and snacks available for movers in appropriate place.

On Move-In Day

- Have camera to record damages.

- Have people ready to (1) check in items, (2) direct items to right place.

- Have water, drinks, and snacks available for movers in appropriate place.

Downloadable TOOL 4.5
On-Boarding Checklist for HR*

Office set up:

_____ Office

_____ Furniture: Desk _____ Table _____ Chairs _____Cabinets
_____ Whiteboard/flip chart _____ Lights

_____ Computer/laptop (with passwords and e-mail access)

_____ Phone/# _____ Cell/#

_____ Employee #

_____ Business cards

_____ Stationary: Pens, paper, notepads, and so on _____ Files

_____ Secretary _____ Administrative assistant

Personal set-up:

_____ Housing

_____ Schools

_____ Spousal assistance

_____ Special needs _____

_____ Cars

_____ Area: Location of stores, recreation, hospitals, transportation routes

_____ Moving company/move assistance

_____ (Driver's license) _____ (Visas) _____ (Language/culture training)

Information/learning:

Information about:

_____ Customers

_____ Collaborators

_____ Capabilities

_____ Competitors

_____ Conditions

_____ Key documents (_____ Bus plan, _____ Financials)

On-boarding conversations: _____ Up, _____ Across, _____ Down

Transition assistance: _____ Orientation, _____ Mentor/coach

Decide How to *Engage* the New Culture

ASSIMILATE, CONVERGE AND EVOLVE, OR SHOCK

Part I—Before you accept a new leadership role: **SELL** yourself first; Do your **DUE DILIGENCE**

Part II—The New Leader's 100-Day Action Plan

Fuzzy Front End   DAY ONE   30   45   60   70   100

You must start BEFORE Day One

Take Control of DAY ONE

Use key MILESTONES to drive team performance

Get the right people in the right ROLES

Decide how to ENGAGE the new Culture

Get buy in for the one BURNING IMPERATIVE and create the new strategy

Invest in EARLY WINS to build team confidence

Shape the team CULTURE with an ongoing communication campaign

Part III—What leaders know:
ADJUST to inevitable surprises; **AVOID** the most common mistakes;
BUILD loyalty, trust, and commitment

There are important choices to be made about Day One. One choice that needs to be made in advance is how best to engage with the existing culture. Cultural engagement is extremely important in a successful transition; and it is essential that an executive know what his or her cultural engagement plan will be before walking in the door for Day One.

When is comes to cultural engagement, it is helpful to think in terms of our ACES model. This model makes a very tricky subject easy. Under the ACES model there are only three cultural engagement choices: (1) Assimilate, (2) Converge and Evolve, and (3) Shock. An executive must pick one of these three strategies and must pick the right one if he or she has any hope of a successful transition. Almost always, it is difficult, if not impossible, to recover from a wrong cultural engagement choice. Picking the right engagement strategy is *that* crucial.

Knowing, in Advance, What Is Going to Be Different

A senior executive from a conservative midwestern consumer products company, went to work in a senior role at a west coast gaming software company. He showed up early on his first day dressed "casually" in khakis and a polo shirt. One of his first questions to his secretary was about what normal working hours were. She replied, "We don't really have any normal working hours. People tend to wander in somewhere between 9:30 A.M. and 11:30 A.M. if they come in. But it really doesn't matter. They're all working 20 hours a day anyway. They're just not doing it here." When people started "wandering" in, the executive realized that he was the most formally dressed person in the place. (His khakis were pressed.) Somewhere in there, he realized just how different things were going to be.

That executive ended up adjusting and helping his new company become even more successful. Still, his start-up could have been even easier if he had thought more about the messages he wanted to send on his first day, during his first week, and during his first 100 days.

Engage with the New Culture— Summary and Implications

Be mindful of how you come in to an organization, using an ACES model to determine whether you want to Assimilate, Converge and Evolve, or Shock the organization with your entry.

We decided to make this a separate chapter to emphasize the need for you to stop and think about how you are going to engage with the culture in general terms after you have completed your on-boarding preparation and before you walk in the door. Listen to everyone, and then trust your gut. It has gotten you this far.

Once you have figured that out, you are ready to tackle the specifics of Day One.

ACES Framework*

A	Assimilate
CE	Converge and Evolve
S	Shock

Assimilating is the safest (not surprisingly). If they wear white shirts, you wear white shirts. If they leave the office at 6:15 P.M. every night, you leave the office at 6:15 P.M. every night. What ever they do, you do. This is the least threatening (and least impactful) approach you can take.

Converge and Evolve is generally a safe middle way that will allow you to move things in the right direction over time. Here you converge with the existing culture first, and then help it evolve over time as appropriate. If they are wearing white shirts, you wear white shirts for a while. Then, at the appropriate time, you evolve into a blue shirt on occasion. (You dare-devil!)

Shock is the opposite of Assimilate. Trying to jump change the culture to your way immediately is the most threatening. There will be active resistance and pushback. The body of the organization will try to eliminate the cause of the changes—you. Thus, this is something you want to do only when you must. If the ship is going down, you must. If there are no controls and the organization is hemorrhaging cash, you must. Just be ready for them to come after you.

CHAPTER 6

Take Control of *Day One*

MAKE A POWERFUL FIRST IMPRESSION

Part I—Before you accept a new leadership role: **SELL** yourself first; Do your **DUE DILIGENCE**

Part II—The New Leader's 100-Day Action Plan

| Fuzzy Front End | DAY ONE | 30 | 45 | 60 | 70 | 100 |

You must start **BEFORE** Day One

Take Control of **DAY ONE**

Use key **MILESTONES** to drive team performance

Get the right people in the right **ROLES**

Decide how to **ENGAGE** the new Culture

Get buy in for the one **BURNING IMPERATIVE** and create the new strategy

Invest in **EARLY WINS** to build team confidence

Shape the team **CULTURE** with an ongoing communication campaign

Part III—What leaders know:
ADJUST to inevitable surprises; **AVOID** the most common mistakes;
BUILD loyalty, trust, and commitment

Our brains remember information "presented first and last, and have an inclination to forget the middle items."[1] People will remember vividly their first impressions of you and their last interaction with you. While you can update their last interaction constantly, you are going to be stuck with those first impressions. So, be choiceful about them. Be choiceful about the messages you send with your words, with your actions, with the order of your actions, and with the signs and

---

[1] Elizabeth Hilton, Differences in Visual and Auditory Short-Term Memory, *Indiana University South Bend Journal, 2001.*

symbols you deploy. This is why Day One is the pivot point for on-boarding. For most people, this is when they will form their first, indelible impression.

Arthur was moving from California to Montana to head up human resources (HR) at a large corporation. When asked what he was doing Day One, he suggested he was going to spend it in an HR orientation. We started to tell him that HR's orientation was less important than on-boarding conversations, but we stopped when we remembered he was coming in as head of HR. So we suggested he redefine Day One.

In the end, Arthur went up to Montana a week early. He used that preweek to meet with some of his key peers. Then, the Friday before he officially started, he met with each of the teams working one of the CEO's top three priorities in HR. And on Monday, he sat through every minute of the HR orientation, brooking no interruptions.

At the end of the day, he bumped into the CEO who asked him how things were going so far. Arthur told him about the meetings with peers and teams as well as his positive impressions of the HR orientation. The CEO could not figure out how Arthur had gotten all that done in one day.

There is no one right way to do this. It is all about the first impression *received*. Different people will draw different impressions of the same thing depending on their perspective and filters. Prior to your first interactions, you will not understand their perspective and filters. So not only is there no one *right* answer, it is going to be difficult to figure out the best answer for your particular situation. This is another reason why it is so valuable to get a jump start on relationships and learning during the fuzzy front end. Not only does that let you manage your initial impressions on those people outside the noise of Day One, it will help you make better choices about your early days.

What Are You Going to Do on Day One?

That question, more than any other, stumps our clients. Once you have gone through the fuzzy front end and you have identified your cultural assimilation plan, what you do on Day One is extremely important because it communicates volumes about you and your intentions. Therefore, you must set the proper tone by doing the right thing on Day One. Of your first 100 days, Day One is often the most crucial. Your Day One may not break your career in your new company, but it certainly can go a long way to sustaining your cause—if you plan it well.

We will give examples of some of our clients' Day One experiences. Remember no two Day Ones will be the same. However, some general principles emerge from these examples:

- *Order counts:* Be choiceful about the order in which you meet with people and the order in which you communicate by listening and sharing.

- *Location counts:* Be choiceful about where you show up for work on Day One. Do not just show up at your designated office by default.

- *Signs and symbols count:* Be choiceful about all the ways in which you communicate, well beyond just words.

- *Day One does not have to match the first day you get paid:* Be choiceful about which day you want to communicate as Day One to facilitate other choices about order and location.

Many of our clients have found value in holding early meetings with as many of the people in their reporting line as they can muster—in person, by video conference, by teleconference, or any other means. These early meetings give everyone a chance to meet the new leader. It does not really matter what the new leader says in this meeting because no one will remember much beyond "hello." And if they do remember, they'll probably remember exactly the parts that the new leader will wish he'd never said. So, we advise new leaders to say "Hello. Nice to be here." and not much else at this point.

Another tool our clients have found valuable is the New Manager Assimilation Session (Tool 6.2 on p. 90). We have included a template for this at the end of this chapter. It is all about killing rumors. It is about getting all the questions that everyone really wants to ask on the table early on in a forum where a critical mass can hear what the new leader has to say at the same time. This prevents person A from filtering the message to person B who filters it again and so on. There will always be rumors. But this process, originally created by Lynn Ulrich of the Jarvis institute and deployed very successfully at General Electric, goes a long way to squelching most of the rumors.

Your Agenda as a Symbol of What's Important

Edgar was joining a company as CEO. He told us the most important thing he had to do was to change the mind-set of the organization to become more customer focused.

"What are you doing on Day One?"

"I've got this planned. I'm showing up, introducing myself to the team, and launching five committees to tackle the five most important priorities."

"What happened to being more customer focused?"

"What do you mean?"

"How does your planned Day One demonstrate that your main goal is to become more customer focused?"

"I guess it doesn't."

"What does it say to your customers?"

"Well, nothing, they won't know about it."

"Exactly."

Edgar's revised Day One: Edgar did introduce himself to the team. But then he said "I'm leaving now. Because, before I'm prepared to talk to any of you about anything, I want to get out and spend some time with our customers."

And he did—10 days. After three days, the chairman called him to express his concern. "What are you doing traipsing around the country? I hired you to run the business."

"I can't do that until I've learned a little about our customers."

After a couple of more days, customers started calling the chairman to tell him how great the new CEO was. "He listens. We're excited about him."

Finally, Edgar came back into the company with a comprehensive understanding of what the customers wanted and knowledge of where his company was falling short. He shared that knowledge with his new team. He met with his direct reports one-on-one to get their perspective on the customers and then used all that information to craft a burning imperative around a customer-centric vision. He took the message forward by calling the top 50 managers together and telling them how the new company imperative was crafted with their input as well as the customers. He explained how the imperative drove the priorities. He said, "Based on our jointly developed imperative, I'm happy to announce the formation of five committees to work on our top five priorities."

Although the top five priorities were essentially the same as he'd originally planned, they contained powerful nuances that better fit the customer needs and his initiative had significantly more credibility because he involved the customers and his staff. His early actions sent a strong communication about the customer's role in the company going forward.

Location Counts

Terry's Arkansas-based company had been bought by a conglomerate a year ago. Now, finally, they were merging his company with another company in Idaho and a smaller company in New Hampshire. We worked with him to map out the communication of the merger and his new role. We all decided that Terry's boss should make the announcement in Idaho with Terry standing right next to him. This was designed to help communicate that this was a merger and not a takeover of the Idaho group by the Arkansas group.

The Power of Signs and Symbols

Thomas had moved from Tokyo to Singapore for a year for tax reasons. During the year, he joined a large bank as head of their Asia group.

"What are you going to do on Day One?"

"I thought I'd go into the office, do paperwork, and start meeting people."

"Which office?"

"Singapore."

"Why?"

"Because I'm here. Why not?"

"Because you're the head of Asia. And the Asian HQ is Tokyo. If you start in Singapore, you'll be perceived as the head of the Singapore branch until you show up in Tokyo in January."

So, instead of starting in Singapore, Thomas and his wife flew to Tokyo and took his direct reports and their spouses out to dinner the night before he started. Then, at 9:00 A.M. Tokyo time, Thomas got on the pan-Asia speakerphone system and introduced himself to his 256 regional employees while standing in the middle of the Tokyo trading floor. Then he met with direct reports during the day. Finally, he took the bank's largest customer in Japan out for dinner to cap off his first day.

Do you see how those actions represent a big difference in terms of signs and symbols? Everything communicates. Showing up to do paperwork in Singapore sends a very different message than showing up and taking charge at the regional headquarters.

Understanding the Culture

Buell was moving into a company as head of marketing. We were on the phone with him and their director of HR. Fresh from Thomas' success in Asia, we suggested a similar dinner with spouses for Buell's team. When the director of HR explained that their company never did anything with spouses, Buell modified it to be dinner without spouses. Different tools for different situations.

Sometimes You Go to the Team and Sometimes You Go to the Boss

Gerry was starting work in London, but most of his direct reports were in Birmingham. He choose to have an office and a secretary and spend Day One in Lawrence because starting in London would make everyone afraid that they were going to have to move there or lose their jobs.

Khalil, however, was coming in to run three divisions. The largest was in Odessa near where he lived. The second largest was in Omaha and the smallest was in Lawrence. His boss's office was in Lawrence. Khalil chose to spend Day One in Lawrence, attending his boss's staff meeting in the morning and then spending the afternoon with the division that reported to him. For Khalil, it was important to signal to his boss that, even though he was living in Odessa, he was going to be available to be part of his boss's team.

Optics Count

Karen was coming into a bank to merge three divisions into one.

"How are you going to get to know the people?"

"I'm in luck. Each division manager has an offsite meeting already planned for my first two weeks. I'm going to use those as a chance to meet the key players and get to know them."

"And that will be the first time you meet them?"

That was the plan. The problem was that this perpetuated the culture of three different divisions as opposed to one combined group. To set a new course, Karen rented a theater for Day One and set it up for video and audio conferencing. Then she introduced herself to the entire staff of the new division at the same time.

She eventually went to the old division's off-sites, but only after setting the stage for the new division first.

Not Communicating Communicates

Kim was coming into a new company as CEO. The old CEO and founder was going to stay on as chief innovation officer.

"Tell me about Day One."

"Oh, I'm all set. I am going to get in early to get my office set up. Then I am meeting with the old CEO from nine to eleven. Then meeting with the CFO from eleven to twelve."

"Are you a hermit?"

"What a silly question. Of course not."

"Well, if I work for you, by noon of your first day I'm pretty convinced you're either a hermit, or shy, or hate people since all you've done is lock yourself in your office."

Instead, Kim called a meeting of the company's top 100 managers at 8:30 A.M. She introduced herself, told everyone how glad she was to be there. She then had meetings with the old CEO and CFO. But, at this point, it was okay because she'd made an initial connection with her team.

Read the Signs—To Suit or Not to Suit?

Jeb got invited to a meeting at a golf club on a Saturday morning. He was told the dress was business casual. But, since he was in Japan, he suspected that might mean something a little different. So he wore grey flannels, a formal shirt, and a blazer.

He was the only one NOT in a suit and tie.

Conversely, Dave joined a company where people dressed casually. I mean really casually: They wore jeans, shorts, T-shirts—to the most formal meetings! After two months, he was still wearing a suit to work. No tie, but the suit trousers and jacket. People thought he was clinging to the armor of his old ways to avoid getting sucked into the culture. He needed to lose the suit. (Or just ship it to the Japanese division.)

So, think about Day One. Think about how you want to learn, how you want to communicate. Do you want to start by meeting your team in the office? Off-site? One-on-one? As a group? Do you want to start with a full-company meeting? Do you want to start with casual meetings? Do you want to start by telling them about you or learning about them? Do you want to start with the team or with customers? From the examples in this chapter, you'll understand that there is no one right answer. But just asking yourself the questions will get you miles ahead of the game. Then think about the next days and weeks and your goals and approach.

HOT TIP

Manage Day One Signs and Symbols: Even though everything communicates, some communication is more important than others. How you spend Day One leaves an indelible impression. Be choiceful about who you spend time with and where. Control the agenda, even if you have to redefine which day is Day One.

Day One—Summary and Implications

At the start a new role, everything is magnified. Thus, it's critically important to be particularly choiceful about everything you do and say and don't do and don't say—and what order you do or say things in.

QUESTIONS YOU SHOULD ASK YOURSELF

- What am I doing on Day One? What does it communicate?
- Am I being choiceful about all the ways I am communicating on Day One?
- Am I making the impression I choose to make on the people I choose to make it on?

Day One Checklist*

Official Day One: _____

Effective Day One in role: _____

Plan entry:

_____

_____

_____

Initial team meeting(s):

_____

_____

_____

New manager assimilation? _____

Other internal stakeholder meetings:

_____

_____

_____

External stakeholder meetings:

_____

_____

_____

External stakeholder phone calls:

_____

_____

_____

Downloadable TOOL 6.2
New Manager Assimilation Session*

The new manager assimilation process gets questions on the table and resolved immediately that would fester without it. This is a very useful session to conduct in the first days or weeks of a new leadership role.

Step 1: Provide a brief introduction and an overview of the objectives of the session and review the process to all involved (team and new manager).

Step 2: Team members, without the new leader present generate questions about:

(i) The new leader (you).

(Professional, personal, including hopes, dreams, rumors, preconceptions, anything)

(ii) The new leader as a team manager.

(What the leader knows about the team, priorities, work style, norms, communication, rumors)

(iii) The new manager as a member of the broader organization.

(What the leader knows about the organization, how they fit, priorities, assumptions, expectations, rumors)

Plus the team should answer the following questions that they'll present to the new leader:

(i) What does the new manager need to know to be successful in new role?

What are the top three issues?

What are the secrets to being effective?

Are there any ideas for the new leader?

(ii) What significant issues need to be addressed immediately?

Are there any quick fixes that are needed now?

Are there any difficult areas of the business that new leader should know about?

(iii) Other questions and ideas?

What is the one question that you are afraid to ask?

What additional messages do you have?

Step 3: New manager rejoins teams to answer questions, listen, and learn.

---

*To customize this document, download Tool 6.2 to your hard drive from www.primegenesis.com/tools.html. The document can then be opened, edited, and printed using Microsoft Word or another popular word processing application.

Get Buy-In for the One *Burning Imperative* and Create the New Strategy (by Day 30)

Part I—Before you accept a new leadership role: **SELL** yourself first; Do your **DUE DILIGENCE**

Part II—The New Leader's 100-Day Action Plan

Fuzzy Front End | DAY ONE | 30 | 45 | 60 | 70 | 100

You must start BEFORE Day One

Take Control of DAY ONE

Use key MILESTONES to drive team performance

Get the right people in the right ROLES

Decide how to ENGAGE the new Culture

Get buy in for the one BURNING IMPERATIVE and create the new strategy

Invest in EARLY WINS to build team confidence

Shape the team CULTURE with an ongoing communication campaign

Part III—What leaders know:
ADJUST to inevitable surprises; **AVOID** the most common mistakes;
BUILD loyalty, trust, and commitment

You can control your schedule during the fuzzy front end—mostly because no one expects you to do anything. You can probably control your schedule on Day One or, at least, have a big influence on it—mostly because no one expects you to have thought it through as much as you have. Your control will be far less over the rest of your first 100 days—because all sorts of people will be putting all sorts of demands on your time. Carving out team building time is going to be tough. But building a high-performing team is essential. So make the time.

On top of everything else you have to do and all the other demands on your schedule, make the time to implement the five building blocks of your team's *tactical capacity*. The starting point, and indeed the foundation, to the development of tactical capacity is the *burning imperative* with its components of mission, vision, objectives, goals, strategies, and values.

Harold was 100 days into his new role as vice president of marketing for a $1 billion manufacturing company when his boss asked him to pick up business development as well. (Harold had handled the initial steps of his complex transition well indeed.) So Harold hit a restart button with the new team, pulling them together for one of our imperative workshops.

They agreed on their mission, vision, objectives, goals, strategies, and plans. Then they got input from some key divisional stakeholders. Then they rolled it up to the division presidents and finally to the CEO who approved the plan. What is extraordinary is not so much what they did as how fast they got it done. From the moment this team first came together until the time the CEO approved the plans was 30 hours. To achieve this, they followed the outline as detailed in the Tool 7.1 on page 111 at the end of this chapter. After its completion, one member of the team said, "I've been here six years. It's the first time I've known what I was supposed to do."

A genuinely shared imperative drives everything everyone does every day. More than any single other factor, this is what distinguishes highly successful teams from teams that flounder and fail. More than any single other factor, this is the key to surviving and thriving in a complex transition. This is the heart of tactical capacity. Teams with a genuinely shared imperative can be more flexible in their actions and reactions because each individual team member can be confident that their team members are heading in the same direction.

Not everyone agrees on how fast you should move to get this in place. The argument for stretching out this process is that the risks of picking the wrong imperative are greater than the risks of moving too slowly. There have certainly been cases where this has been true. If things are going well, there's less urgency to change things. But we all have seen that the pace of change is accelerating as information flows more and more freely. In that environment, even if things are going well, there are going to be competitors converging on your position rapidly. Thus, you need to move quickly. Today, it is better to get moving and adapt as appropriate. How fast should you move on this? Very fast. Get this in place by the end of your first 30 days.

The core elements of a team's burning imperative are mission, vision, objectives, goals, strategies, and values. These drive the team's actual plans and actions.

Burning Imperative

Mission: Why are we here? Why do we exist? What business are we in?

Vision: Future picture showing what do we want to become; where are we going?

Objectives: Broadly defined, *qualitative* performance requirements.

Goals: The *quantitative* measures of the objectives that define success.

Strategies: Broad choices around *how* the team will achieve its objectives.

Values: Beliefs and moral principles that guide attitudes, decisions, and actions.

People often confuse the difference between a mission and a vision. Sometimes people just combine the two. But they are different. A mission guides what people do *every day*. It informs what roles need to exist in the organization. A vision is the picture of *success in the future*. It helps define areas where the organization needs to be best in class and helps keep everyone aware of the essence of the company.

Mission

Simply put, a mission statement informs the organization about how to spend its time. However, mission statements are often so complex and convoluted that they do not have meaning to anyone. The best mission statements are concise, clear, and motivating. They leave no question as to the "higher good" or the "ultimate focus" of the organization.

Here are some examples of mission statements that do that well:

- "Provide relief to victims of disasters and help people prevent, prepare for, and respond to emergencies." *American Red Cross*
- "Win the Tour de France." *Lance Armstrong's Discovery Bike Racing Team 2005*
- "Improve the lives of the world's consumers." *Procter & Gamble*
- "Give ordinary folk the chance to buy the same thing as rich people." *Wal-Mart*
- "Solve unsolved problems innovatively." *3M*
- "Get the Apollo 13 Astronauts back to earth alive." *NASA during the crisis*
- "Bring happiness to the world's families." *Disney*
- "Preserve and improve human life." *Merck*
- "To explore new worlds, discover new civilizations; seek out new life forms, and to boldly go where no one has gone before." *Starship Enterprise*

These missions inspire people. Note that all of these missions have a verb. They are all about being called to do something: explore, seek, go, give, bring, solve, preserve and improve, provide, help, respond.

Let's look at some real mission statements that do this less well:

- "Total customer satisfaction."
- "Increase shareholder value."
- "Constant improvement in products and services to meet our customers' needs."

It is not that there is anything technically wrong with these. It is hard to argue against the ideas of increasing shareholder value, customer satisfaction as a good thing, or constant improvements. It is just that these could apply to any organization. There is unfortunately nothing truly meaningful about them. And these were from large companies that should have the sophistication to know better:

- "Total customer satisfaction." *Avis*
- "Increase shareholder value." *Coca-Cola*
- "Constant improvement in products and services to meet our customers' needs." *Goodyear*

Now, not all companies will have a higher calling like the American Red Cross. Some organizations define themselves in terms of their competition or a benchmark.

- "Yamaha o tsubusu." (Utterly waste and destroy Yamaha.) *Honda*

Missions like this motivate people in different ways, but they still work. Honda's mission led to a great focus over time. While Honda never accomplished its stated goal of destroying Yamaha, targeting Yamaha helped Honda grow and gave its employees a focused sense of competition to fuel that growth.

It is worthwhile to invest the time to create a strong mission statement that helps everyone be clear on what they should be doing every day.

A Mission Story

The Coca-Cola system is the world's largest producer, marketer, and distributor of non-alcoholic beverages. There are over a million people working in the system in over 200 countries and multiple companies. All together, it's one of the most powerful commercial juggernauts ever assembled. In many ways, everyone in the system knows what they are trying to do. In other ways, they are disconnected and spend more time competing within the system than competing with organizations outside the system.

The Coca-Cola Company's stated overall *mission* was to "Increase shareholder value." But to the local Coca-Cola Company team in Nigeria, this was not all that helpful. They saw the statement as a way to keep score, not guidance for what to do every day. The team decided that as far as they were concerned, The Coca-Cola Company really existed to "refresh the world's consumers." Now this was something they could use to guide their actions. They focused their efforts on figuring out ways to "refresh"

Nigeria's consumers and this led to revenue and profit growth and shareholder value increases.

Vision

A good vision is an appealing picture of future success, showing what the company will be like when the mission is accomplished. Some examples of clear and inspiring visions:

- "The world's premier engineering organization. Trained and ready to provide support anytime, anyplace. A full spectrum engineer force of high quality, dedicated soldiers and civilians." *U.S. Army Corps of Engineers*
- "Create a world-renowned, yet personable, showcase of maverick films, filmmakers and the technology that enables creativity." *Cinequest*
- "A world in which every child, everywhere, has equal access to life-saving vaccines." *The Vaccine Fund*
- "The preeminent global manufacturer and marketer of power tools and accessories, hardware and home improvement products, and technology-based fastening systems." *Black & Decker*
- "Bring the world into the jet age." *Boeing* (1950s)
- "Become the Harvard of the West." *Stanford* (1940s)

Some examples of less clear and less inspiring visions include:

- "A dynamic and successful company that is founded upon and operates solely through the principles of Respect, Integrity, Trust, Communication, and Honesty (RITCH)." *Reynolds & Reynolds*
- "Achieve superior return on assets while consistently increasing revenue." *Greif*
- "Good place to work. Company with a future." *Bradley*

The differences between these become apparent when you imagine yourself in the shoes of an agent of each of these visions. If you work at:

- The U.S. Army Corps of Engineers, you know you must invest in the engineer force to be ready to support it when needed.
- The Vaccine Fund, you know you are investing in getting life-saving vaccines to children.
- Stanford in the 1940s, you know you are striving to converge on everything about Harvard except its location (and climate).

On the other hand, if you showed up for work at Reynolds & Reynolds, Greif, or Bradley and were given the vision statement, you would probably be less sure what the company's real priorities were, and, as a result, clueless about how to spend your time and or to channel investment.

J. D. Power and Associates' primary business is customer satisfaction surveys. But its *vision* for the automobile industry is "Improved automobile quality." The publicity J. D. Power and Associates has generated over the years behind its surveys has sparked just that. J. D. Power's Associates are far more excited about the improvements they helped drive on the way to achieving the vision, than they are about the mechanics of their surveys.

It is worthwhile to invest in creating a good vision statement so that everyone is clear on where the organization needs to become best-in-class versus just good enough. For most things, good enough is all that is required and investing extra time and resources to become better than good enough is superfluous. For the areas required to achieve the vision, the organization needs to be meaningfully better than anyone else is and needs to invest to maintain and grow that lead.

Objectives are the broadly defined, qualitative performance requirements of the business. Examples include achieving market leadership, dominating a category, and so on. Objectives should be closely related to the company's vision. If the vision is "A world in which every child, everywhere, has equal access to life-saving vaccines," the objectives might be: (1) creation of vaccines, (2) manufacture of vaccines, (3) awareness of vaccines, (4) funding for vaccines, and (5) distribution of vaccines.

Goals flow out of objectives. Goals need to be SMART (Specific, Measurable, Attainable, Relevant, and Time-Bound). Objectives do not need to be SMART since they inform the goals. For example, if the main objective is creation of vaccines, the current year's goal could be to develop three market-ready vaccines by June 30. The topic of goals will be covered in Chapter 8. For now, you just need to know that they follow, rather than lead, objectives.

Some organizations flip the definitions of objectives and goals with goals being the more broadly defined and objectives being the specific, measurable part. That works too. Just make sure the team is clear on the general direction and how to measure success.

Strategy is about the creation and allocation of resources to the right place in the right way at the right time over time. By corollary, there is a wrong place, a wrong way, and a wrong time. So, strategy boils down to selecting which options to pursue and which options not to pursue. As Michael Porter puts it, "Strategy is choosing what not to do."[1] Choosing not to do something that is stupid is easy. The tough choices come in choosing not to pursue an option that is a good idea—but for someone else or at a different time. We drive strategic choices with two questions: Where is it that we want to play? How will we win in the area? Simple and focused. If you want or need more, see Appendix I on strategic planning (pp. 197–206).

Values are the beliefs and moral principles that guide actions and decisions—these are things that a team cannot walk away from to pursue its mission and vision. Value-driven teams do *not* believe the end justifies the means. Values are important to them because values guide both individuals and teams on a day-to-day basis.

Anyone can stop any Procter & Gamble discussion dead in its tracks by asking: "Are we doing the right thing?" If they are not doing the right thing for their customers, suppliers, employees, communities, and owners, they change. There's a strong service component running through Procter & Gamble's DNA. They often do things that are right for consumers with little or no regard for the short-term financial implications. Many companies today wish they had done this in the past so that they could have Procter & Gamble's reputation in the present. But they did not and do not.

The problem with many corporate values statements is that they use empty words that sound nice but don't drive choices. Take, for example, the following values statement from one large company. It could be almost any company, which is exactly the problem:

---

[1] Michael Porter, *Harvard Lecture.*

Respect: We treat others as we would like to be treated ourselves. We do not tolerate abusive or disrespectful treatment. Ruthlessness, callousness, and arrogance don't belong here.

Integrity: We work with customers and prospects openly, honestly, and sincerely. When we say we will do something, we do it; when we say we cannot or will not do something, then we won't do it.

Communication: We have an obligation to communicate. Here, we take the time to talk with one another . . . and to listen. We believe that information is meant to move and that information moves people.

Excellence: We are satisfied with nothing less than the very best in everything we do. We will continue to raise the bar for everyone. The great fun here will be for all of us to discover just how good we can really be.

If values are driving choices through the organization so people know what to do, the values are useful regardless of what particular values the company chooses. However, if they are not driving choices, they are useless. Moreover, if the values statement includes values that are not really valued, the statement will be counter-productive because people will see the missed-match between words and actions and then question leaders' other words as well. (Enron's value statement in the 1990s arguably helped contribute to the confusion that led to its demise.)

It is worth the effort to create a precise and accurate value statement so that everyone is clear on the beliefs and moral principles that should guide their actions and decisions.

Let's go back to the NASA Apollo 13. At "Houston, we've had a problem . . ." the mission changed from rolling around on the moon and collecting rocks to getting the astronauts home alive. This was a burning imperative that trumped all other worries and galvanized the entire team. Everyone knew they had to focus on this and put aside all the distractions of petty office politics, worrying about raises, promotions, or time off, and anything else that would get in the way of the imperative.

You may not be able to come up with an imperative that is as clear and compelling as this, but you need to make it as clear and compelling as you can. The more clear and compelling it is, the higher the likelihood that the team will understand it and strive to deliver it.

The Case of Multiple Purposes

The 200 people at Internet development firm Guidance Solutions were split into two groups. The core, first part of the company, was focused on delivery. Its leaders had built the company to the level it was by providing superior service to existing clients regardless of cost. They were convinced that their past success resulted from doing this and that they would continue to be successful going forward in the same way. Why worry about profits? They never had worried about them in the past when everything worked out in the era of the Internet boom during which value was not related to profits. Value was derived from customer satisfaction.

The second part of the company had been brought in to grow revenue. The CEO had originally joined the company to head sales. He used to say that sales consisted of holding his order pad out the window and waiting for customers to sign up. That had worked for a couple of years. The company was operating at capacity and they'd just attracted a large outside investment.

But, the collapse of the NASDAQ in April 2000 signaled the beginning of the end of that. Now, the CEO knew he had to turn his deal evaluators into deal creators and build a real sales team to attract profitable clients.

But he and the company's president, who had founded the company and now headed "delivery," never pulled the two parts of the company together with a shared imperative. As a result, the two parts continued on their merry way with the sales/business development group bringing in more and more clients with a goal of trying to maximize profitability while the delivery group tried to maximize effectiveness and deliver near perfect technology solutions. But to what end? Each of these key groups was successful on its own, but as a whole the organization failed because the two groups were operating with different missions in mind.

Making It Happen

There are a number of different ways to put together mission, vision, and value statements. We have used one-day imperative workshops with great success. Tool 7.1 on page 111 is designed to help you and your team reach consensus on your mission, vision, objectives, strategies, and often values in a single, day-long session. The operative word is consensus. You probably already have a mission, vision, objectives, strategies, and values in your head. They may even be down on paper. Your team may have told you they agree. But, do they really believe them? Do the mission, vision, objectives, strategies, and values really drive their actions? Is the imperative really shared?

Peter Senge lays out different ways of rolling out ideas: telling, selling, testing, consulting, and co-creating.[2] The premise behind the one-day workshop is to create the imperative with your core team so it is truly shared by all. Then, roll that out by letting others in the organization consult with your core team. You should be open to wording changes and some new ideas during the rollout but preserve the meaning of the burning imperative that you and your team created together.

This is better than trying to let the entire organization create its imperative because doing that requires so many compromises that you're likely to end up with something that is acceptable to most and inspirational to none. By creating with just your core team, you can lead the team toward more choiceful, inspirational ideas.

Done right, an imperative workshop is an intensive session with a lot of personal sharing and dialogue. Expect to learn a lot about your team. Expect them to learn a lot about you. It is possible that you'll end up with an imperative very close to what you came in with. It is more likely you won't. Even if you do, there's power for all in the learning. As T. S. Eliot says in Little Gidding:

We shall not cease from exploration.
And the end of all our exploring
Will be to arrive where we started
And know the place for the first time.[3]

---

[2] Peter Senge, *The Fifth Discipline*, London: Century Business, 1990.
[3] English poet T. S. Eliot, "Little Giddings," *Four Quartets*, Orlando, FL: Harcourt Brace Jovanovich, 1943.

Imperative Creation Variation—Consulting

Lionel, a new leader, wanted to make a big impact quickly. But he knew his direct reports couldn't lead the broader team to where it needed to be. So he opted for a consulting approach to building a shared imperative. He drafted it and then shared it with people one by one over a period of a couple weeks, collecting their input and incorporating it as appropriate. When he was done, he took a planned change approach to deploying it:

- Sent written document out to team.
- Read key parts of document to team at team meeting two days later.
- Reinforced key messages during that two-day team meeting.
- Reinforced key messages at the next sales meeting.
- Reinforced key messages at all staff meetings.

A few months later, Lionel hired a senior vice president of sales. He recognized the need for an imperative for the sales department and, in this case, the sales directors were sophisticated enough for Lionel to use a workshop approach. This had the advantage of accelerating the rollout. His approach:

- Workshop Wednesday/Thursday
- Final notes to team Monday (leaked to next level down by design)
- Subteam meetings Wednesday to roll out imperative
- "All-hands" call on Friday so everyone could hear the imperative from the new sales vice president

This case gets even better. The senior vice president of sales invited the new senior vice president of marketing to his team's workshop. The marketing senior vice president was so impressed with what he heard that he used the same mission statement to kick off the marketing workshop. This allowed them to spend less time on crafting a mission and more time on thinking through priorities and the implementation calendar. Additionally, the marketing senior vice president was able to include some key people from other departments in his workshop to start developing buy-in with them as well.

Another Imperative Workshop Variation

John pulled together his direct reports during his first week on the job for an imperative workshop. He took the team offsite to a local sports club for the day and brought in a professional facilitator. Before the meeting, no one had ever written down a mission, vision, or set of values for the division. It is not that there was any disagreement about them. It is just that no one had ever thought about them.

The facilitator had John begin by laying out his take on the corporate mission—"fulfill consumer needs around the world"—and his vision for the division. Then the facilitator had each member of the group, including John, break away and put together a personal shield depicting answers to key questions that John had asked in hopes of everyone getting to know each other better. Thirty minutes later, they came back to share the pictures and words they had put together.

The sharing was remarkable in that most of these people who had worked together for long periods, in some cases for years, all learned new things about each other. People were amazed at Su's description of the village she was from in the heart of China and the descriptions of her extended family in that village. Others were awed by the story of the secret present Sven's father gave his near destitute neighbor after the feast of St. Lucia. Of course, no one was surprised when Janet talked about her pride in putting together and selling a small manufacturing company so quickly after college. She had told many of her colleagues that story before.

After the sharing, the group moved over to the bowling alley for some heated competition and a pizza lunch. They spent the couple of hours there mulling over what they had heard, talking to each other about what they had learned about each other, and trying to convert spares.

When they finally got back together, the facilitator had translated the stories from the shields into values. Su's village and family story got translated into "mutual support." Sven's St. Lucia's festival gift story became "doing the right thing even when no one else knows." Janet's company creation story became "getting noticed and appreciated." There were over 50 different values on the flipcharts to which the group added a couple of dozen more in a matter of minutes.

Then the facilitator helped them combine values that were similar and group them into buckets. It was a relatively easy and uncontroversial exercise because the shield stories had helped people understand why some values were so important to their colleagues. In the end, the group came up with five core values that they all agreed were important to them. They were:

1. *Pursuit of mastery:* Relentless efforts to inspire, motivate, and create new standards of excellence and grow to new levels of performance in everything we do, every time we do them. Get the right things done right and never settle for average results.

2. *Integrity:* Whole people, acting from the same principles, values, and personal priorities in all situations. Intellectual honesty and apolitical, uncompromising straight talk where words match beliefs and actions match words—firm, fair, and courteous.

3. *Diversity:* Seeking different perspectives and ways of doing things to find the third way. Working closely together with a common cause, over-communicating and taking the time to break down the barriers and listen actively with compassion and patience.

4. *Courage:* Daring to initiate and lead, to boldly explore new ideas, to seek out and fearlessly embrace the inevitable mistakes and missteps as learning opportunities.

5. *Optimism:* Choosing to find the bright side of things, be enthusiastic, enjoy what we do, celebrate the successes, learn from the failures, keep our sense of humor, and have fun.

They had reached consensus on this. While this clearly was not the list that any individual member of the group would have written on their own, they all felt good about the team's values and felt they would all be better off if they each used these to guide their behaviors.

The mission discussion was even easier. Since this division was focused on Peru and focused on snacks, the corporate mission was translated to "fulfill consumers' snack needs in Peru."

And the vision discussion was easier still. They took what John had talked about earlier and modified it a little. They decided their picture of success was simply "the highest snack market share of any corporate division in the world." Given their cost structures and business model, they knew that achieving this would result in correlating profit success.

Finally, they translated that vision into a single mid-term objective and goal: To grow, from their current 25 percent market share to a 35 percent market share in three years.

They left excited. They had learned about each other. They felt great about the shared values and had a shared clarity around where they were headed. And the team felt very good about John. He had struck the right balance between leading and being part of the team. He laid out his vision early on and then allowed the team to improve on it. He laid out his personal shield like everyone else. The group knew that ever after, the people who had been at this session would have a special bond.

Learning: John successfully used an imperative workshop to get his core team to co-create a shared imperative: mission, vision, objective, goal, and values.

Commit or Quit

Dorothy used an imperative workshop to help her board members decide whether to commit or quit. Dorothy was president of a local not-for-profit organization. The national organization had adopted a new mission statement and was requiring the local chapters to adopt it as well.

In the course of the workshop, it became clear that several of the members of the board fundamentally disagreed with the national mission.

"That's not relevant here."

"I can't ask my friends to give money to an organization with that mission."

In the end, the board decided to fold the entire organization into another local organization, abandoning the national brand name along with its mission.

Arriving at a Different Place

Not all workshops end up back at the place that you started. Monica was charged with creating a marketing innovations group. Her opening statement at the workshop laid out what she envisioned for the group and how she wanted its people to come up with innovations beyond just marketing communications. The mission was "system innovations."

But the consensus of the group was that there was room for more. After some debate, the group changed the mission to "incubating ventures capable of becoming a full-time job for someone." This then drove their thinking about resources and staffing to "venture managers in residence." The idea was for people to come into the group and work on a range of innovations until they found the one they wanted to take to market as a full-time job. Innovations not capable of that were dropped.

Preemptive Strike

Cal's company was acquiring another company. Since the department comparable to his in the acquired company was larger than the group he ran, he decided to do a preemptive imperative effort. (We've reached new heights of jargon here. If "preemptive imperative" doesn't make you laugh, you're taking all this way too seriously.)

He used an imperative workshop to get his existing team clear on their future mission, vision, and priorities.

Then he took that output and shared it with his boss and the merger team so they would know what he was planning to do.

After the merger, Cal was put in charge of the combined group because he was the man with the plan and his team was in better shape than was the acquired group.

What Do You Want? What Are You Willing to Give Up to Get It?

Not unlike any other organization, Randy's new sales team was busy. He did not want to distract them from their "real work" of selling. So he found a way to fit the imperative work into the existing processes.

First he drafted an initial imperative on his own.

Then he shared it with his direct reports and their teams during the course of account reviews.

Finally, he modified portions of an already-planned sales meeting to get input into the revised imperative and get people to buy in.

In the end, he got to the place he needed to get to a little slower than he might otherwise have done, but with less disruption to the current state of affairs.

Coming Together

Marge had a different issue. She was merging two groups who hated each other. So she called an imperative workshop. But the real goal was to give the two groups a chance to vent their issues. Once they had done that, a shared imperative practically fell out of the discussion.

HOT TIP

The Burning Imperative: This is the centerpiece of tactical capacity. When people talk about getting everyone on the same page, this is that page. Use whatever methodology you would like to get it in place. But get it in place and get buy in early. Very early.

The Case of the Flailing Team

Procter & Gamble was being attacked by Lever Brothers on three fronts at the same time. Lever had recently launched a fabric softener, Snuggle, to compete with Procter & Gamble's category leader, Downy. They had launched a dish detergent, Sunlight, to compete with Procter & Gamble's category leader, Cascade. And they had launched a washing detergent, Surf, to compete with Procter & Gamble's category leader, Tide. Moreover, in each case, the Lever brands were priced 9 percent below the Procter & Gamble leader.

Procter & Gamble's senior management was concerned. So they spent more time than usual in understanding the three brands' defensive postures. As always, it came down to basics:

- Redouble efforts to drive product and packing improvements. Over the long run, consumers value superior performance and delivering superior performance was always the key to long-term success.
- Increase advertising spending. Actually, the key was not so much actual superior performance as it was perceived superior performance. Actual performance was essential but it had to be communicated clearly and persuasively.
- Match pricing and promotions over the short term to minimize share loss.

These three Procter & Gamble brands followed these tenants, launched product, and packaging improvement efforts, increased advertising, and matched Lever's pricing. Then Lever dropped its pricing again to stay 9 percent below the Procter & Gamble brands. And when Procter & Gamble matched that, they dropped their pricing again. Clearly, this was a major attack.

Procter & Gamble's senior management was committed to securing these brands' position. So they moved some of their best people over to the brands and redirected short-term funding to invest in them.

And it worked. While Lever got a toehold and built strong brands, Procter & Gamble maintained its position as market leader in these three categories.

But not in bar soap.

Lever's objective all along had been to secure category leadership of bar soap. In bar soap, they had a superior performing product—Dove—and a number of other strong brands and exciting innovations like Lever 2000. As Lever looked at its range of strategic options, they chose the option of distracting Procter & Gamble. Their theory, which worked, was that if they attacked some of Procter & Gamble's related and highly profitable brands, Procter & Gamble would focus on defending those and take its collective eye off bar soaps.

Workshop Attendance and Timing

In the real world, you'll be taking over an existing team with existing priorities and existing schedules. It's not likely that your team members will have planned to take a day out of their "real" work to sit around, hold hands, and sing *Kumbya*. First point, this is real work and the imperative workshop tool is focused on real business issues. It does end up being a strong team-building exercise itself, but as a byproduct of the work. Even so, there will be some team members who are reluctant to adjust their existing schedules to accommodate this workshop, particularly if you push to hold it sometime in your first 30 days.

Stick with the plan. Find the date in your first 30 days that works best for most people and then give the others the option to change their schedules or not. This approach has two advantages:

1. It keeps things moving forward in line with the 80 percent rule. Not everything is going to be perfect. Not everyone can be at every meeting. You and your team will move forward as best you can, helping others catch up and adjusting along the way.

2. It gives you early data about different team members' attitudes. Everything communicates. And everything communicates both ways. Inviting people to an imperative workshop sends a powerful message. Turning it down because they have something more important to do sends a different message.

Burning Imperative—Summary and Implications

The *burning imperative* is the cornerstone building block of tactical capacity. Everything pivots off a business's mission, vision, values, and objectives:

Mission: Why are we here, why do we exist, what business are we in?

Vision: Future picture—What do we want to become; where are we going?

Objectives: Broadly defined, *qualitative* performance requirements.

Goals: The *quantitative* measures of the objectives that define success.

Strategies: Broad choices around *how* the team will achieve its objectives.

Values: Beliefs and moral principles that guide attitudes, decisions, and actions.

For the burning imperative to drive everything everyone actually does every day, it must be truly shared. Thus, you should strive to get it in place and shared early on.

QUESTIONS YOU SHOULD ASK YOURSELF

- Have we laid the right foundation on which to build a high-performing team?
- Have we identified a burning imperative?
- Is it compelling enough to the key stakeholders?
- Do we have a strategy and plan to make it real?

Imperative Workshop*

This is a one-day, off-site workshop to drive consensus around shared mission, vision, objectives, goals, strategies, and values. *All* members of the core team must attend. This workshop will determine the team's burning imperative.

Preparation

- In premeeting communications, set a clear destination for the meeting (mission, vision, objectives, goals, strategies, and values).

- Set context—current reality—broader group's purpose.

- Send invitations, set logistics.

- Prepare to present your current vision (leader); prepare to explain your role (team members).

Delivery

- Detail the destination: framework, mission, vision, objectives, goals, strategies, plans, values (facilitator).

- Present the current vision (team leader).

- Present the current subgroup roles (team members).

- Set up what's important.

- Review the corporate/larger group purpose (team leader).

- Complete the personal shields exercise to establish personal and group values (facilitator).

- Revise the team's mission, vision, objectives, goals, strategies, and plans in turn by encouraging an open, but focused discussion to expand ideas, group them into similar categories, select the ones that resonate with current vision, rank them in order of importance, solicit individual drafts, collect common thoughts, create a group draft based on input (facilitator).

- Discuss how the new burning imperative is different from the old situation (facilitator).

(continued)

- Summarize what it will take to achieve the burning imperative (facilitator).
- Wrap up and tie the results back to the destination and communicate the next steps.

Follow-Up

- Share with broader team for their input.
- Make refinements if required.
- Communicate the final results to all key stakeholders.
- Live it. Use as basis for all other work.

CHAPTER 8

Use Key *Milestones* to Drive Team Performance (by Day 45)

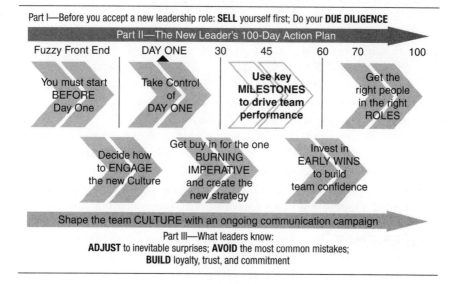

Part I—Before you accept a new leadership role: **SELL** yourself first; Do your **DUE DILIGENCE**

Part II—The New Leader's 100-Day Action Plan

Fuzzy Front End | DAY ONE | 30 | 45 | 60 | 70 | 100

You must start BEFORE Day One

Take Control of DAY ONE

Use key **MILESTONES** to drive team performance

Get the right people in the right ROLES

Decide how to ENGAGE the new Culture

Get buy in for the one BURNING IMPERATIVE and create the new strategy

Invest in EARLY WINS to build team confidence

Shape the team CULTURE with an ongoing communication campaign

Part III—What leaders know:
ADJUST to inevitable surprises; **AVOID** the most common mistakes; **BUILD** loyalty, trust, and commitment

Milestones are the building blocks of tactical capacity; they turn a burning imperative into manageable chunks. Done right, your team's milestone management practice will be a powerful team reinforcer itself. This is all about follow through. In brief, drive clarity, specificity, and linkages and then move the focus from individuals to team.

Sam's team put a lot of time and energy into creating a shared imperative during a two-day workshop. They left excited and ready to move forward. Then Sam got busy and never put in place the milestone management process. As a result, the team quickly went back to doing things the way they'd been doing them before. If Sam wasn't going to follow through, why should they?

The real test of moving from strategy through to tactical capacity lies in the actual practices that are set up among team members. Tactical capacity implies, by definition, that significant leeway should be built into practices. A team who has internalized its imperative—mission, values, and objectives—and developed a keen sense of mutually assured success, will have a real foundation for true tactical capacity, and will be able to do what it takes to succeed, even if that means adapting and modifying aspects of the initial plans that were laid out. There should be nothing mechanical about this aspect of preparing for and executing a complex transition. It requires nuance, insight, close monitoring, and collaboration.

Practices enable people to implement plans. Practices need to be coupled with systems of metrics and rewards that reinforce the desired behaviors. There is an old saying: "Show me how they are paid and I'll tell you what they really do."

John Michael Loh, U.S. Air Force Air Combat Command during the first Gulf War said: "I used to believe that if it doesn't get measured, it doesn't get done. Now I say if it doesn't get measured it doesn't get approved. . . . You need to manage by facts, not gut feel."

Specific performance measurements free people and teams to do their jobs without undue interference and provide the basis for nonjudgmental discussion of performance versus expectations and how to improve. It is essential that people know what is expected of them and have the time and resources they need to deliver those expectations.

NASA and the Apollo 13 ground team provide another good example of this. The imperative of getting the astronauts back home alive was compelling, but overwhelming. It was easier to work through the milestones one by one:

- Turn the ship around so it would get back to earth.
- Manage the remaining power so it would last until they were back.
- Fix the carbon-monoxide problem so the air remained breathable.
- Manage reentry into the atmosphere so the ship didn't burn up.

You can encourage people to do what you really want them to do by clarifying:

- How their individual roles fit with the broader group
- Individual SMART goals (Specific, Measurable, Attainable, Relevant, Time Bound), in writing
- The resources and guidelines required for success
- The link between performance and consequences
- The supporting actions and milestones along the way, in writing

Fit with the Broader Group

Goals *must* fit with big picture: They must reinforce and work in conjunction with the established values, mission, and vision. Furthermore they must coincide with the overall strategy and the specific priority actions detailed in the strategic plan. This is a tall order and the importance should not be underestimated.

One research company had spent its time pursuing market share. They were investing in wooing their competitor's clients and, on occasion, even bought out some of their competitors. Then, finally, they did some market research and discovered that they had an 83 percent market share but that only 20 percent of their target customers were using any research services at all. Since it was going to be far easier to convince new users to join the category than to convert a meaningful quantity of their competitors' clients to switch, that is what they did. Obviously, it was important to realign everyone's goals to this.

SMART Goals (Specific, Measurable, Attainable, Relevant, Time Bound)

It's simple. If you want your goals to have relevance, they should conform to *every* element of the SMART structure:

Specific—Concrete objectives are easier to achieve and track.

Measurable—If you cannot measure it, you cannot manage it.

Actionable/**A**ttainable—Things you can make happen or influence (and can achieve).

Relevant—To your overall mission and plan.

Time bound—Including milestones along the way.

Wharton Professor Len Lodish says, "It is better to be vaguely right than precisely wrong." We fully subscribe to this theory in most cases. When it comes to goals though, it is all about precision. Without SMART measurements in place, it is impossible to understand how people did. With precision, the judgmental debates go away. One manager used to insist that his 8-year-old daughter be able to understand how people did versus their objectives at the end of the period. He figured if people could make goals so clear and straightforward that an 8-year-old could understand performance versus the goals, they wouldn't be arguing about them come review time.

Required Resources

Just as it is important for people to understand how their goals fit with the rest of the organization, it is equally important to make sure people have the resources and support (internally and externally) they need to achieve their goals. For example, it would be silly to ask the salesforce to sell 100 widgets per day with plant capacity of 50 per day. You would end up with unhappy customers, furious salespeople, and nervous breakdowns throughout the plant.

To help reinforce the creation, deployment, and achievement of goals, you need some assistance. That assistance comes in the form of five reinforcements: skills, knowledge, tools, resources, and guidelines:

1. *Skills:* These are the "how to's" or capabilities. Your goals may be perfect, but you will not reach them without the necessary skills in place. Know what those skills are and which ones you have to develop.

2. *Knowledge:* This boils down to what you are aware of in terms of facts and experiences. The greater your breadth and depth of knowledge, the higher your chance of reaching your goals.

3. *Tools:* Without the right equipment, you cannot reach your goals. You must know what equipment is needed, what you have, and how to fill the gap.

4. *Resources:* The three key resource needs are: human, financial, and operational. Make sure that resources that are available to support your established goals match in each of these areas. If not, you either have to change your goals to make them more realistic, or increase your access to the needed resource.

5. *Guidelines:* Establish boundaries so everyone knows how far they can roam. Know the things that you cannot do.

Link between Performance and Consequences

As many organizations get larger and more bureaucratic, they tend to bunch people's annual raises in a narrow range, doing things like giving those that meet expectations 3 percent to 5 percent raises and those that exceed 4 percent to 6 percent raises. Over time, this has a devastating effect on performance because people see that they are not going to be rewarded for putting in extra effort to overdeliver and won't get punished for marginal underdelivery.

Make the link between performance and consequences explicit. If that link is properly established, the ratings should be self-evident at the end:

- For example, goal: $100MM in sales.
- 120+ is "exceeds."
- 105 to 120 is "meets and exceeds."
- 95 to 105 is "meets."
- 80 to 95 is "marginally meets."
- Below 80 is "below."

One organization decided that the average raise for the year was going to be 4 percent. No problem there. But then they let their employees know that 4 percent was the average target. This created problems because the people who got "meets expectations" ratings had been told there was nothing wrong with that rating so they expected to get the average raise. And the people who got "above" and "exceeds" ratings expected raises well beyond the 4 percent. To compound the problem, less than 5 percent of the people in this organization got ratings below "meets." So the math didn't work. As a result, this company did not establish a clear and valid link between performance and consequences. By giving 40 percent of the people a 4 percent raise, and 55 percent of the people a greater than 4 percent raise, the organization could not possibly meet their average goal of 4 percent. When this organization broke that link, they also broke the team's motivation to excel.

Actions and Milestones along the Way

You cannot do mid-course corrections if you do not know where you're supposed to be at the mid-course. It is far easier to spot a problem when someone says "we produced 9 widgets last month versus a goal of 30," than when someone says "we experienced normal start-up issues but remain fully committed to producing 360 widgets this year." Laying out milestones is critical for understanding how to redeploy resources over time to achieve the overall goals.

For example, if a CTO has a goal in February of installing a new database by September that will provide twice the capacity of the existing one, his key milestones might look something like this:

- Potential vendors identified by 3/1 (status: completed 2/15).
- RFPs issued by 5/1 (sent out 4/15).
- Proposals in 7/1 (expect by 6/15).
- Decision made 8/1 (committee meeting scheduled for 7/15).
- Database installed 9/1 (expect to be two weeks early).

Case Study—The Importance of Clear Goals

The good news was that the division's people did have goals in place. There were two problems though. First, none of the goals were measurable. Second, everyone thought that any rating below "above expectations" was a failing grade.

The goals that were established included:

- Successfully manage team.
- Service clients.
- Provide support to sales group.

Clearly these goals did not follow any of the SMART guidelines previously discussed.

The rating scale was:

- Exceeds Expectations
- Above Expectations
- Meets Expectations
- Marginally Meets Expectations
- Below Expectations

There is nothing wrong with this ratings scale. The issue was that almost no one got the bottom two ratings, about 40 percent of the people got a "Meets" rating, 40 percent got an "Above" rating, and 20 percent got an "Exceeds" rating. So the median fell somewhere in the "Above" category.

During John's first time through the review cycle, almost everyone thought they deserved an overall "Above" or "Exceeds" rating. People said "I managed the team more successfully," "I serviced my clients really well," and "I provided superior support to the sales group." One of the people in John's organization had received a "Meets" rating on each one of their goals. Even this person's overall rating was "Above." John suggested that the overall should be "Meets." When the person being reviewed saw that change, she objected vehemently. "But," she said "achieving all the goals has always been rated Above."

John decided not to push too hard for the changes on this first review cycle. Instead, he made sure everyone had SMART goals in place for the next review cycle and made sure everyone understood how results versus those goals would translate into overall ratings. He then went on to make sure everyone had measurable quarterly milestones in place so they could tell how they were doing throughout the year.

Learning: Specific, measurable goals and a consistently applied ratings scale can take a lot of the conflict out of performance reviews.

The Case of the Great Programs

Jack, the head of marketing, was convinced that innovation was the key. On brands that promised excitement, their programs needed to

be exciting. And since many of the brands were huge, the team had
money to spend to make sure the programs and promotions had a
huge impact as well. Thus, the only mistake was in thinking too
small. So Jack built a team of big thinkers.

They delivered. On one promotion, they gave away 500,000 soc-
cer balls. On another, they gave away 2,000,000 winning game tickets. Their in-pack promotions had higher winner/nonwinner ratios
than any other company's. They supported the promotions with
massive amounts of custom-developed media advertising. The group
consistently delivered new, innovative, exciting programs.

Jack rewarded the team for their efforts. Raises were strong.
Bonuses were high. Life was good.

But, the business was flat.

Combined volume on the brands was the same as it had been
four years before. Worse, the increase in promotional spending had
almost offset the modest price increases they'd been able to push
through the system. Profits were up, but nowhere near what had
been hoped for.

Jack's replacement, William, came in and looked at the history
of the programs and promotions. When he asked what worked, he
was presented with numbers about reach, redemption rates, and
cost per prize, total prizes redeemed, and the like. No one was able
to tie any of the programs to volume impact. Thus, no one was able
to calculate program profitability either. This was partly because
there were no promotion tests done, partly because there were no
"clean" base periods, and partly because they were running multiple
programs at the same time.

William decided the first step in being able to measure results
was to create the "versus" to measure results against. So he can-
celled all consumer promotions for a 12-month period. William
knew this was going to be painful, but he needed to clear a readable
base so they could test promotions' impact versus a control and the
base to understand their real impact.

The gods of unintended consequences had fun with William
during that year. Instead of running consumer promotions, William
put all his money into trade promotions/retail pricing and advertising. The brands' market shares grew and volumes were up.

At the end of the year, with volume and profits up, the team
started testing promotions. Some grew business profitably. Some
did not. But, now with a "versus" established they were able to figure out which was which.

Group Milestones

Lars believed in the power of the milestone process and implemented it with his team. He followed a simple milestone reinforcement strategy that constantly reinforced the importance of milestones to the team. He attempted to do this using a three-step method:

1. As milestones were updated, he circulated them to the team in advance of its meetings.
2. He started every meeting with a five-minute roundtable where every team member could discuss his or her milestone progress.
3. He then spent the second half of the meeting focusing on the most import issues driving the milestones.

Lars got the team to lay out the milestones and put together updates in advance. But he asked questions and encouraged discussion during the five-minute updates. So he never got to the second half of the meeting. Good, but not good enough.

The next week, Lars held everybody to their five minutes and restrained himself from weighing in during those parts. The team was able to get to the most important issues in the second half of the meeting and have better, more complete, conversations about those issues. Better.

Milestone Management at the Board Level

Garr's board meetings were out of control. Individual board members kept taking the group off the meetings' agendas in order to emphasize their own favorite issues.

To combat this, Garr put in place a milestone management process. Each board member submitted his or her updates to the board secretary ahead of the board meeting. The secretary then compiled them and sent them back out to everyone at least 48 hours in advance of the board meetings.

At the two-hour board meetings, the first hour was spent with each of the 24 board members giving a two-minute recap of their updates, emphasizing the areas where they needed help or thought more discussion was warranted.

At the halfway point, the board president looked at all the outstanding issues and ordered them from highest priority to lowest priority.

The board spent the next hour working through the issues in priority order, not worrying about time. They never got through the entire list in meetings. But that was okay because the issues they got to were more important than the issues that had to be discussed later.

This revolutionized the board meetings. Everyone got two minutes in the spotlight. Everyone got a chance to raise issues. But the agenda was no longer managed on a first-come first-serve basis. As a result, the board was able to spend more time on the more important issues.

HOT TIP

Use Milestones as a Way to Build the Team: The goal is to set up a self-regulating system of control points. You need everyone looking at the same metrics in the same way. You want progress to be transparent so you are doing as little judging of *individuals* as possible (i.e., the job of the metrics) and as much leading and helping the *team* as possible.

Driving Team Performance

Done right, much more management time should go into helping people create and achieve their goals and milestones than in reviewing them. There are two phases to this. The first is goal creation. The second is support and encouragement.

Upfront investment in getting the right goals in place always pays back more than the investment. For people to develop and commit to the right goals, they need to know how their role fits with what others are doing; be confident they've got the right skills, knowledge, tools, resources, and guidelines; know the positive and negative consequences of their performance; and have a plan to achieve the goals.

All of that is necessary, but not sufficient. There needs to be a process in place to track performance and redeploy resources, as appropriate, to respond to changing conditions along the way. Rolling quarterly planning (RQP) is a good way to do this.

The essence of RQP is getting the team together once per quarter, in the middle of the quarter. At these meetings, the team will:

- Review learning from the previous quarter.
- Look at the current quarter's progress and discuss the best allocation of resources for the balance of the quarter.
- Lock into the next quarter's milestones and resources.
- Look at evolving plans for future quarters.

People can use the goal recording and tracking sheet (Tool 8.1 on p. 125) as a tool for the RQP process. People fill them in for the year, laying out their milestones, the person responsible, and timing for completion—of each milestone on the way to the ultimate goal or subgoal.

Then, before each quarterly meeting, they update the status on each milestone. For milestones still in progress, they lay out what help they need from others on the team. For milestones that have been completed (or abandoned), they should lay out the learnings. This information gets circulated before the meeting so that everyone has time to read everyone else's pages. Doing this allows the discussion in the meeting to focus on learnings and help/linkages. Instead of talking about who achieved or did not achieve what milestones, the group talks about what they can do together to optimize future performance.

Thus, we suggest the following steps for putting in place and implementing a performance management system:

1. Discuss how the person's role fits into the bigger picture.
2. Agree on base goals and stretch SMART performance goals.
3. Agree on the required skills, knowledge, tools, resources, and guidelines.
4. Explicitly link performance and consequences (rating, bonus, raises, and so on).
5. Establish actions for success—How goals will be accomplished, milestones.
6. Summarize in writing to confirm mutual understanding and commitment.
7. Deploy a mutually supportive team-based follow-up system that helps everyone improve their performance versus goals (like RQP) with meetings like this:

- Circulate individual milestone updates to the team to read in advance of each meeting so you can take update sharing off the agenda.
- Use the first half of each meeting for each team member to headline their wins, learning, and areas in which they need help from other team members.
- Use the second half of the meeting to discuss the overall team's most important issues and opportunities re: milestone delivery.

Milestone—Summary and Implications

1. Clarify how individual roles fit with broader group/objectives.
2. Put in place SMART goals:

   Specific

   Measurable

   Attainable

   Relevant

   Time bound
3. Give people resources and guidelines to enable success.
4. Communicate and deliver on the link between performance and consequences.
5. Track actions and milestones along the way with process that optimizes performance going forward.
6. Manage the process to drive *team* milestones and priorities as opposed to individuals.

QUESTIONS YOU SHOULD ASK YOURSELF

- Is everyone clear on who (roles) is doing what (goals), when (milestones) with what resources?
- Is there a system in place to manage milestone achievement so I do not have to do it myself on an ad hoc basis?

Downloadable TOOL 8.1
Goal Recording and
Tracking Worksheet*

Group Milestones	Who	When	Status	Help Needed
Priority programs:				
Capabilities:				
Process:				

Prior to meeting:

• Each team member submits their update.

• Updates compiled and circulated prior to the meeting.

At meeting:

Each team member gives five-minute update during the first half of the meeting including:

• Most important wins,

• Most important learnings, and

• Areas they need help on

Leader orders topics for discussion in priority order at half-way point.

Group discusses those topics in that order during second half of meeting, spending as much time as necessary on each one.

Remaining topics deferred to next meeting or separate meeting.

CHAPTER 9

Invest in *Early Wins* to Build Team Confidence (by Day 60)

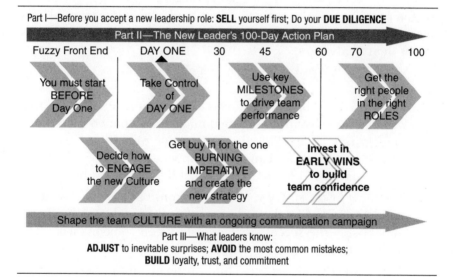

Part I—Before you accept a new leadership role: **SELL** yourself first; Do your **DUE DILIGENCE**

Part II—The New Leader's 100-Day Action Plan

| Fuzzy Front End | DAY ONE | 30 | 45 | 60 | 70 | 100 |

You must start BEFORE Day One

Take Control of DAY ONE

Use key MILESTONES to drive team performance

Get the right people in the right ROLES

Decide how to ENGAGE the new Culture

Get buy in for the one BURNING IMPERATIVE and create the new strategy

Invest in EARLY WINS to build team confidence

Shape the team CULTURE with an ongoing communication campaign

Part III—What leaders know:
ADJUST to inevitable surprises; **AVOID** the most common mistakes;
BUILD loyalty, trust, and commitment

There is often a conversation about six months after a leader has started a new role. Someone will ask the new leader's boss how the new leader is doing. You have probably taken part in these conversations before.

"By the way, how's that new leader Rhonda doing?"

"Rhonda? She's fabulous. Love the intelligence. Love the attitude. She may be off to a slow start. But what a great hire! Really like her."

Result: Rhonda's probably on the way out, or, at the very least, in real trouble. Rhonda may not find out about it for another 6 to 12 months but her boss's "off to a slow start" sealed Rhonda's fate. Compare that versus:

"Rhonda? Let me tell you about all the things she's gotten done. . . ."

Rhonda's made. Of course, Rhonda has not done it all herself. Her team has. But Rhonda was able to get the team focused on delivering early wins and by doing so gave her boss something concrete to talk about.

Early wins give the leader credibility and the team confidence—two very good things. For NASA and Apollo 13, fixing the oxygen problem was the early win that made the entire team believe they could succeed and gave them the confidence to deal with the rest of their challenges.

Our prescription is relatively simple:

1. *Pick one or two of the milestones as early wins.* Pick things that will make a substantial external impact and that your boss will want to talk about. Pick things that you are sure you can deliver. Pick things that can model important behaviors. And pick things that would not have happened if you had not been there.

2. *Pick them by the end of your second month* so you and the team can deliver them by the end of your sixth month. This will give your bosses the successes they need when someone asks how you are doing.

3. *Over-invest to over-deliver.* Think in terms of massing your resources against a point. Do not skimp on your early wins. Put more resources than you think you could ever justify against these early opportunities so you and your team deliver them better and faster than anyone could have ever thought possible.

Get to Where the Puck Is Going

Pamela was hired to lead marketing for a major office equipment supplier. She and her team did a nice job of getting the imperative and milestones in place. Then it was time to pick an early win. She picked redesigning the trade show booth.

Her logic was that there was a major trade show coming up in a few months and all her senior management would be there. To get a new trade show booth in place right would require redoing the marketing strategy, positioning, branding, and brochures along the way.

So she managed the project herself while effectively engaging her team along the way and delivered a superior product in record time.

Senior management was blown away by the booth. It was tangible, real, and impactful. It was far better than what they had before and clearly something they never would have gotten without Pamela. Great early win!

Championing the Champions

Oscar decided to focus his efforts on four projects. He reached into his organization to pick four "champions" to drive them and then gave them extra help on-boarding into their new roles, extra support, and extra resources.

Three of the projects produced early tangible results. One did not do so well.

But the three that did well were enough to turn the whole business around. The division Oscar had been brought in to run had been declining by 1 percent every month for 24 months, as it did for Oscar's first two months. Then, in month three, it was up 1 percent. In month four, it was up 4 percent. In month five, it was up 10 percent.

No one even bothered asking how Oscar was doing in month six. Everybody knew because the numbers told the story.

Redefining Success

Quincy did not like this early win concept at all. His issue was that he was leading a recording division in which it was going to take 12 to 18 months to deliver anything. To him, delivering a meaningful early win in his first six months seemed impossible.

So, we helped him rethink how he defined early wins.

He borrowed the pipeline concept from pharmaceutical companies and created a recording pipeline. On Day One, the pipeline was empty. But, by month six, he had a whole bunch of viable projects in the pipeline and was able to show that to his senior management as a measure of success. His early win was showing tangible momentum toward a longer-term goal.

HOT TIP

Over-Invest in Early Wins: This is the key to dealing with the early delivery landmine. You never have as much time as you think. It usually takes more resources than you think. Getting an early win is about survival for the new leader and renewed confidence for the team. It is that important. So over-invest in it accordingly.

Charter the Team

Because the early win is so important for the confidence of the team, it must be driven by the team. You, as the leader, can direct, support, and encourage. But it can't be your win. It must be the team's win. Thus, the most important things you can do are set the team up for success and support its efforts. This all begins with a team charter.

Tool 9.1 on page 134 will help you develop this. Its key components are:

- *Objectives/goals:* Specific, measurable results
- *Data:* Information they'll need to be successful
- *Guidelines:* What the team can and cannot do
- *Resources:* What they will have to deliver their objectives
- *Accountability:* What and how

Early Win—Human Vending Machines

Coca-Cola's Hong Kong team did a three-day strategy workshop. Chuck worked with outside facilitators for about six weeks pulling it together and then stepped out to let the selected team go through the workshop on their own after setting the task. The task was to figure out how to increase Coca-Cola's beverage penetration of Hong Kong's housing estates. Doing this would help move the overall business toward its 35 percent market share goal.

The team doing the work included Coca-Cola's local head of marketing, head of product supply, and head of alliances; two Coca-Cola people from a different country; the heads of sales and of marketing at Coca-Cola's local bottling company; the creative director of a local advertising agency; the owner of a local wholesale distributor; and two local consumers recruited by a research agency.

The session began in a restaurant in one of the local housing estates. There the facilitator laid out the objectives of the three days and gave the participants a hint of what was to come. After lunch, the facilitator sent the participants off in pairs to spend the afternoon with families in the housing estates. Their assignment was to reconvene at 8:00 P.M. and tell the others what they had noticed.

The groups came back full of observations. Within a half an hour, there were hundreds of notes on flip charts with observations about shopping, living conditions, cooking, family meals, and all sorts of other aspects of family life in a Hong Kong housing estate.

For the excursions the next day, the group was continually shuffled so different members worked with each other. In each case, the pair would go out with a translator and a driver who knew how to get them where they needed to be—and back. The excursions included a trip around Hong Kong in a helicopter to get a different perspective on the housing estates; a mid-day session with teens either on the beach, at the movies, playing basketball, having lunch, and so on; a couple of hours working in a "Wet Market" selling fish, meat, vegetables, and other produce.

After each excursion, the group reconvened and recorded what they'd noticed. Finally, at the end of the day, they had over 1,000 notes on the wall and the facilitator had them select the few that were most "intriguing." Through a series of exercises, they got down to five ideas they wanted to explore for increasing Coca-Cola's beverage penetration in the housing estates.

The next morning, the team regrouped to turn those ideas into a strategy. They had learned a couple of important things:

1. Hong Kong's families in housing estates were generally made up of three generations, six to eight people living in 400 square feet.

2. There were no elevators in the housing estates.

3. All generations liked Coca-Cola's brands and drank them outside of the estates.

The idea that emerged was primarily a distribution idea. Figure 9.1 shows what they presented to Chuck at noon that day:

The team was very excited about their idea. The core of it was to use one family on each floor to sell Coca-Cola's beverages to the other families on the floor. Coca-Cola would give the local stores a 20 percent discount on beverages sold to the distributing family. The stores would pass the discount on to the families who would then sell the beverages to their neighbors at exactly the same price the local stores sold them for. The team also thought Coca-Cola should introduce new brands and stronger advertising over time.

Remember the composition of the presenting team. It included a couple of key people from Coca-Cola as well as key people from their bottling partner and outsiders to inject fresh perspective.

FIGURE 9.1   **Plan for Distribution**

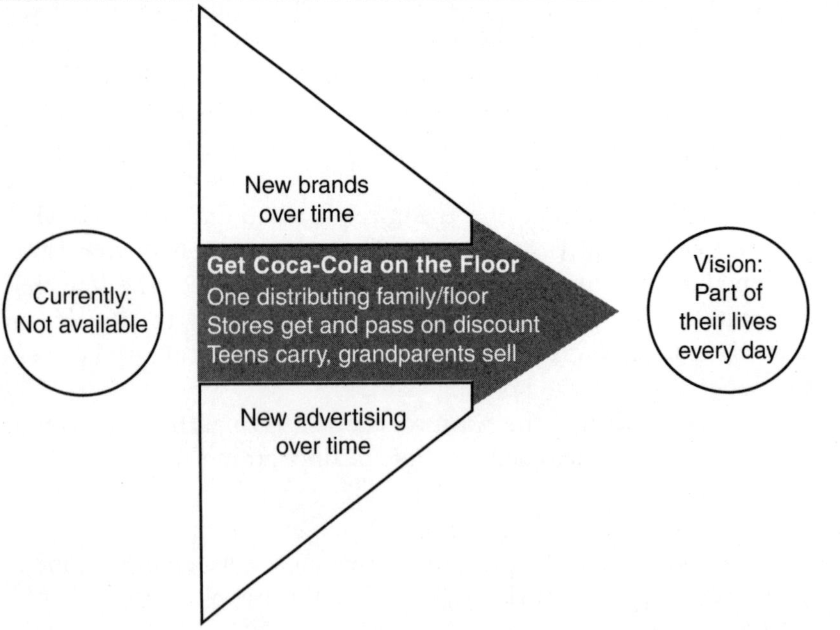

Currently:
Not available

New brands
over time

Get Coca-Cola on the Floor
One distributing family/floor
Stores get and pass on discount
Teens carry, grandparents sell

New advertising
over time

Vision:
Part of
their lives
every day

Chuck, the new division head, was listening to live consumers' advice on strategy.

Learning: Chuck used a strategic planning workshop to do two things: (1) Generate a breakthrough strategy in line with the burning imperative's mission and vision, and (2) get his team and their main ally/customer to work closer together in line with the burning imperative's values.

Early Win/Plans—Summary and Implications

Early wins are all about credibility and confidence. People have more faith in people who have delivered. You want your boss to have confidence in you. You want the team to have confidence in you and in themselves. Early wins provide that confidence.

QUESTIONS YOU SHOULD ASK YOURSELF

- Have I identified an early win that will accomplish all that it needs to in terms of securing my job and giving the team confidence?
- Do I have confidence in the subteam's strategy and tactical capacity to deliver this win?
- Am I certain that I have invested enough resources to accomplish the win?

Team Charter Worksheet*

Useful for getting teams off to the best start on their way to an early win:

Objectives/goals: Charge the team with delivering specific, measurable results.

_____

_____

Data: Provide the information that led to objectives; consumer, customer requirements.

_____

_____

Guidelines: Be clear with the team what they should and should not do, their scope, constraints, how they can add members, how they can implement process changes, and how the responsibility grid works (in terms of who recommends, approves, consults, or provides input).

_____

_____

Resources: Be clear with the team what resources they have in terms of members, leader, mentor, facilitator, other people/consultants, experts, budget, and equipment.

_____

_____

Accountability: Be clear on accountability structure, update timing, completion timing.

_____

_____

CHAPTER 10

Get the Right People in the Right *Roles* (by Day 70)

Part I—Before you accept a new leadership role: **SELL** yourself first; Do your **DUE DILIGENCE**

Part II—The New Leader's 100-Day Action Plan

Fuzzy Front End   DAY ONE   30   45   60   70   100

You must start **BEFORE** Day One

Take Control of DAY ONE

Use key **MILESTONES** to drive team performance

Get the right people in the right ROLES

Decide how to **ENGAGE** the new Culture

Get buy in for the one **BURNING IMPERATIVE** and create the new strategy

Invest in **EARLY WINS** to build team confidence

Shape the team CULTURE with an ongoing communication campaign

Part III—What leaders know: **ADJUST** to inevitable surprises; **AVOID** the most common mistakes; **BUILD** loyalty, trust, and commitment

We are going to push you hard in this chapter. We are going to make you feel uncomfortable by suggesting you make people move faster than you've been used to doing. You certainly do not have to follow our advice on timing. But, you should at least understand it for those times when you will need to follow it. And don't get distracted by the timing debate. Getting the right people in the right roles with the right support is a fundamental, essential building block of a high-performing team. Without the right people, there is no team.

Getting the right people in the right roles is guided by the team's mission, vision, and values, as well as by individuals' strengths. The mission determines the ideal organization—what roles are required to do the things that need to be done on a daily basis. This gives you a map of what roles you need to have—and what roles you do not.

Southwest Airlines is in the business of transporting people by airplane. Their organization needs to include people to maintain the planes, fly the planes, sell tickets, and service their passengers. They need these roles. They do not need chefs, bartenders, or masseuses— even though some other airlines do have people like that.

With a picture of required roles in hand, you can now look at which roles will have the greatest impact on achieving your vision. The roles responsible for these tasks are the critical ones. The other roles encompass tasks that can be done merely "good enough." This is where strategy and people overlap—determining which roles need to be best-in-class and invested in, and which roles can be just maintained or outsourced.

The airline industry, as an industry, loses buckets of money over the long term. (This is true for most industries centered on transporting people.) Yet, Southwest makes money every year. Part of why they do that is that they have figured out which are their critical roles. Southwest over-invests in maintenance roles so they can turn their planes around faster. They over-invest in training their stewardesses and stewards so passengers' in-air experience is fun. Conversely, they under-invest in food service and on-the-ground waiting spaces.

The NASA team members on Apollo 13 were aligned around a clear burning imperative, had clear milestones, and got a big early win by fixing the oxygen/carbon-monoxide problem. While everyone was willing to do whatever it took to get the astronauts home safely, they stayed in their roles. One group of physicists figured out how to wrap the spacecraft around the moon and get it going in the right direction. Another group of engineers fixed the oxygen problem. Another group dealt with the reentry calculations. And the spare crew truly did whatever it took to try things out. They were all working together without getting in each other's way.

Strengths

Now, you are ready to match the right people with the right roles. Marcus Buckingham and Don Clifton's core premise is that people do better when they capitalize on their own, individual *strengths*—talent, knowledge, and skills.[1]

Strengths are necessary for success. But they are not sufficient. People must want to do well and they must fit in. It is helpful to think in terms of strengths, motivation, and fit.

Motivation

Motivation tends to come out of a match between the day-to-day activities of the role and things the person filling the role likes to do. In the end, all people are volunteers. They will choose to give their best efforts where four sets of needs are satisfied: compensation, employability, meaning in the work, and share in shaping the destiny.

Compensation includes financial and nonfinancial rewards, recognition, and respect. Short-term compensation like salary and benefits are purely hygiene factors that need to be competitive in the field to keep people from worrying about them. They need to be good enough to get people to show up for work. Incentive compensation like bonuses and commissions can be tied to line-of-sight performance to motivate people around critical efforts. And long-term compensation like stock, amazingly enough, are designed to keep people mindful of the long-term effects of their actions.

All these are financial rewards. But nonfinancial rewards like recognition and respect are critical motivating factors. The leader of one business made it a point to take every associate who earned a top performance rating to lunch in the month after performance reviews. He would sit down, chat for a while, and then tell him how appreciative he was with all his contributions. Then he would ask him to tell him about what he really did. In each case, the person just lit up! Just asking people to talk about the good things he or she does is one of the best ways going to recognize people.

Employability is all about learning and development. Very few people think they are compensated at the level they truly deserve. Many of them accept less than ideal compensation because they believe they will earn more down the road. These people look to their current jobs to improve their employability by giving them improved

---

[1] Marcus Buckingham and Donald Clifton, *Now Discover Your Strengths*, New York: The Free Press, 2001.

knowledge or skills that will improve their resumes. This is a good thing. It means there is a short-term benefit to investing in training and development as well as a longer-term benefit because people value the learning on its own. This is the whole premise behind low pay or no pay internships.

The U.S. armed forces does this particularly well with its service time for education trade-offs. People who join the armed forces while they are in college get all their expenses paid in return for a commitment of time to the service. These people can extend the deal through various graduate schools by just adding time on to their service commitment. For many, this is a way to get an education and training they could not afford otherwise.

Meaning in the work goes straight back to the burning imperative. Many people want the satisfaction of making an impact on others, having interesting work, or just enjoying what they do. Even if their own individual task does not make a direct impact, people feel good if they know how their task fits into what the organization does and know how the organization as a whole is making an impact on others. (Sounds like mission and vision to us.) Others derive satisfaction just from what they do on an everyday basis.

This is obviously true for professions like teaching, social work, nursing, research, and so on. But it's an important factor in almost any job. For many, it is the difference between showing up from 9 to 5 and really engaging in the work. You can get a good reading of peoples' commitment by what they are thinking about in the shower. When you are getting attention during people's shower time, they are probably finding meaning in the work.

Share in shaping the destiny is about influence and being informed. Few people expect to make all the major strategic decisions in an organization. But people want to be heard. They will feel better if they believe they are well informed and have a seat at the table where decisions that directly impact their work lives are made.

The best way to make them feel this way is to keep them informed and give them a seat at the table. Recall our suggestions for creating the burning imperative. We argued against the total organization co-creating it, but argued for letting others consult. This is an example of giving people influence even without decision-making authority.

Fit

Fit comes out of perspective, values, and biases. Perspective, in turn, comes out of how people have been trained to view and solve business problems. This is the accumulation of people's business experience as manifested in their mental models. For example, people with a classic "sales" perspective may feel they can sell any product to customers. Conversely, people with more of a marketing perspective may feel the organization should modify its products and services to meet customers' needs. We are not suggesting that one is better than the other, just that they are different perspectives.

We talked about values in the section on imperative. It is rare for all of any individual's values to match all of the organization's values. However, it is important for most of the core values to match and for none of them to be in direct conflict with each other.

Different people work in different ways. Some roles may require people with a greater sense of urgency. Some roles require people who think things through more thoroughly before jumping in. Putting someone who tends to get a later start on the day in the role of making morning coffee for the group before everyone else comes in would force that person to work in opposition to his bias and would most likely be a recipe for failure (and bad coffee).

The Case of Delayed Realignment

It is a classic tale. It was the seventh game of the 2003 American League Baseball Championship Series. The winner moved on to the World Series. The New York Yankees, perennial winners and their pitching ace Roger Clemens versus the Boston Red Sox with 86 years of disappointment and their pitching ace Pedro Martinez.

Fourth inning: Clemens is struggling. Yankee manager Joe Torre takes him out—early, decisively, without a lot of discussion.

Eighth inning: Martinez is struggling. Red Sox manager Grady Little goes out to the pitcher's mound and asks if Martinez has "enough bullets in (his) tank." The response: "I have enough." Little leaves him in. "Pedro wanted to stay in there," Little said. "He wanted to get the job done, just as he has many times for us all season long." As Martinez put it, "I would never say no. I tried hard and I did whatever possible to win the ballgame."

Martinez and the Red Sox proceed to blow the lead and lose the game. Once again Clemens, Torre, and the Yankees go on to the World Series while two weeks later, Little loses his job.

As the sportswriters put it, Little's decision was "based more on loyalty and emotion than logic." From Torre's point of view, "In game seven, you've got a short leash. I'd worry about his emotions after the game."

There is a lot in common between game seven and a complex transition. Everyone is on a short leash. So it's essential to move early and decisively.

How One Bad Apple Spoiled the Batch

Zach was head of marketing for the division. He knew he was being considered for a new role so he created a deputy head role to groom his replacement. Then he was able to convince his long-time colleague Cathy to move from her home country to fill the role and eventually take his place.

The good news was that Zach got his new role six months after Cathy showed up. The bad news for Cathy was that the authorities decided to bring someone in from another company as head of marketing instead of giving it to Cathy.

Betty showed up as the new head of marketing and was charged with a classic complex transition; turning around the business in a new company, a new industry, and a new country. The good news for her was that she had Cathy, a well-respected deputy in place to ease her transition. Or, so she thought.

It was never clear whether Cathy was actively trying to sink Betty, whether Cathy thought she was making things easier for Betty, or whether Cathy was simply doing what she'd always done and was clueless about the impact her actions were having on the organization. But Cathy chose to share as little information as she could with Betty and make as many decisions on her own as she could.

Betty spent a lot of time one-on-one with Cathy trying to build an emotional bond. After a few months, she began to suspect that something was amiss and started spending more and more time with Cathy's direct reports to build her own direct bridges and network. She was reasonably effective in this, was able to keep things going without any major disasters, and avoided directly confronting Cathy.

Despite Betty's best efforts, things weren't turning around. With Cathy as an impediment, Betty had to spend more time working the team than she should have and thus spent less time managing the business. Additionally, she was not able to get a clear read on Cathy's team to make the people moves she needed to make.

All that changed six months into Betty's new role. The global head of marketing called Betty into his office and told her straight: "You're not moving fast enough on your people. I want you to go back and fire Maurice and Pat (two of Cathy's direct reports). They're not helping."

On the plane back, Betty thought things through and decided not to fire Maurice and Pat. Their issues were that they were in the wrong jobs. So she moved them to new roles within the division and started procedures to move Cathy out of the company.

Betty cut out a layer of management, got the team excited about her new direction, and made a huge impact on the business. Eighteen months later, the global head of marketing promoted both Maurice and Pat into new roles in corporate headquarters.

This story and the story of the Yankees beating the Red Sox in the American League Championship Series make the same point. You have to do what is right for the organization *and* what is right for the individuals. You have to find a way to get the right people in the right roles at the right time. You have to do it early and decisively. You should worry about their emotions—but never let emotions interfere with making the right decisions at the right time.

90 Feet from Hero to Goat

This case, related to us by our partner Mark Hubbard, took the right person out of the right role and put him into the wrong role. Many baseball fans consider Johnny Bench to be one of the greatest catchers ever to play the game. (Those of you that are not baseball fans are probably a little sick of the baseball analogies in this chapter. Bear with us. This is the last. And it is a good one.) Late in Johnny's career, his knees started hurting and catching was becoming more difficult. The manager, knowing that Johnny could still provide a punch at the plate, not to mention team leadership, wanted Johnny in the lineup, so he moved him to third base. Not having any recent experience in that role, Johnny was terrible at third base, committing errors constantly. It's still baseball, the new role was just 90 feet away, yet what seems like a simple move (probably not to base-ball fans) can take someone from being the best in the business to being the worst in the business.

Once you have someone in the right role, leave them there and support them in that role. Also, remember that just because some-one is good in one role doesn't mean they'll be good in another role that requires different strengths and motivations.

Cut the Pain Out Early

Connie had never been sure of Andrew. She was going to make a de-cision about him "in due time." Then Andrew confided to a facilita-tor at one of Connie's meetings during the break, "You should know I don't trust Connie. I think she screwed me out of a promotion and is out to get me."

There is an old adage that you cannot trust someone who doesn't trust you. Connie's "due time" had arrived.

Cut the Pain Out Early (Or, at Least, as Early as Practical)

Sherman had just taken over as general manager. He knew he had to improve both the sales and marketing functions dramatically as soon as he could. He knew he had to replace the heads of both func-tions in their current roles. But he also knew that both were ex-tremely valuable, respected, and valued employees who could make important contributions in other roles.

What Sherman did, that still seems to have made sense, was to begin recruiting for their replacements immediately, while building strong personal relationships with them and working to figure out other roles for them.

Fast-forward six months. Sherman put new heads of sales and marketing in place. He kept the old heads of sales and marketing as direct reports, but he put them in new, more appropriate roles that enabled them to make important impacts on the organization and actively help their replacements succeed.

How Fast Should You Move on the Team?

In general, you need to have your plan in place to sort roles and make people moves at the end of 70 days or 10 weeks. There are going to be some times when you need to move much faster. And there are going to be times when it takes you longer to implement the plan. But the 70-day target for figuring it out is bound on either side by some things to consider.

There is a risk in moving too fast. The risk is that you'll make poor decisions and come across as too impulsive. By the 70-day mark, you will have had a chance to see people in the imperative workshop, in the milestone management process and, some of them, in the early win kick off. At the 70-day mark, you can make your decisions based on past reports and on your own observations. Thus, 70 days doesn't seem too fast.

There's a larger risk in moving too slow. At about 100 days, you own the team. Once you own the team, the problem children become your problem children. You can't blame them on your predecessor any more. And the other team members may see moves on them as evidence that you don't fully support the team. Furthermore, the other team members know who the weak links are. The number one thing high performers want is for management to act on low performers so the whole group can do better.[2] If you move too slowly, the other team members will wonder what took you so long.

To be clear, you will likely not be able to implement your decisions all at once. You may need to put in place transition plans, supporting weaker team members or strong team members in the wrong roles during the time it takes to get their replacements on-board and up to speed. We're not suggesting you make all your moves in your first 70 days no matter what. We are suggesting you have the plan in place and begin making moves as appropriate.

HOT TIP

Move Faster on the Team: Have a bias to move faster on your team than you think you should. The risks of moving too fast are nothing compared to the multiplier effect of leaving people in the wrong place too long.

---

[2] Thanks Dave Kuhlman of Sibson Consulting for this insight.

Performance/Potential

Putting the right people in the right roles is a key driver of success. The heart of this tool is a grid that matches people with roles (Tool 10.1 on p. 148). The grid is based on two dimensions: performance and potential. Mapping people on this grid then helps inform decisions about which people are in the right roles and which are in the wrong roles so you can support some and move others. This is a simple but highly effective tool for thinking about a complex subject.

The performance measure is drawn from an individual's last or current review/assessment in their current role. It is driven by results versus goals.

The potential measure is a correlation of the strengths, motivations, and fit required for the role they are in and their own strengths, motivations, and fit. The role's strengths, motivations, and fit should be drawn from position descriptions. The individual's strengths, motivations, and fit could be drawn from their latest review, Gallup's StrengthFinder,™ or another assessment questionnaire or tool.

Every organization has its own way of doing position profiles. The better profiles include the key elements of the mission, strengths, motivation, and fit. One way to do this is to answer the following questions in each of the specified areas:

Mission

- What is the mission for this position? Why does it exist?
- What are the responsibilities associated with the role?
- What are the desired objectives or outcomes of the position?
- What impact should the role have on the rest of organization?

Strengths

- What are the *talents* required to achieve success in the role? (Consider talents to be a recurring pattern of thoughts, feelings, or behavior that can be productively applied.)
- What are the *skills* required to achieve success in the role? (Consider skills as the how to's, or the steps of an activity. They can also be identified as capabilities that can be transferred such as technical, interpersonal, or business skills.)

- What is the *knowledge* that is required to achieve success in the role? (Consider what the role holder needs to be aware of or know. What is the required education, experience, and qualifications?)[3]

Motivation

- How do the activities of the role fit with the person's likes, dislikes, and job criteria?
- How will the person progress toward long-term goal? What will drive them or keep them focused?

Fit

- Does the person's values fit the team's?
- Does the person's style and character fit well with the company or team's style and characteristics?
- Does the person's style and character mesh with the supervisor's working style and characteristics?

Structure

Structure is about how the organization is designed and set up—reporting relationships, financial structure, and, increasingly important, the information structure. Structure exists to facilitate plans and practices. As such, it needs to flow out of an organization's mission and strategy.

The key guiding words on structure are "necessary" and "sufficient." Organizations must have in place the structure necessary to manage businesses' operations, information, and finances. But, any more structure and layers of management than is sufficient quickly becomes waste. Extra structure is like insurance. You only want to insure what you cannot afford to have happen. Too many layers and too much structure choke an organization.

Once again, tactical capacity is the ability to assure that operational, informational, and financial structure flows out of and reinforces the organization's mission and strategy. Time and again we

---

[3] The strengths definitions are drawn from Buckingham and Clifton's book *Now Discover Your Strengths*. See note 1.

have seen examples of companies that build up operational structures based on a vision of success rather than a vision of how to get to that success—putting the cart before the horse—and ending up sabotaging the entire project with unforeseen costs, inflexibilities, and other deadly burdens.

Coca-Cola's China Division had paid little attention to Taiwan. They managed the business out of their Hong Kong office and gave their local distributor tremendous freedom. The good news was that the distributor had a superb general manager on the ground and things were going well. The company was concerned about what would happen when that general manager moved on to other things. So the company put a team in place in Taiwan focused on consumer marketing and in-store marketing execution.

Coca-Cola made a couple of structural choices in this that flowed out of their strategy and mission. The strategy of using company people to ensure the gains made by the local distributor were sustained led to putting a team in Taiwan. The mission "to refresh consumers in Taiwan," led to those people being consumer experts and in-store marketing experts. Thus, the mission suggested which positions needed to be in place somewhere and the strategy dictated which got more emphasis. The two together suggested it was less important to put in place a Taiwan-dedicated finance, information technology, or media team than to put in place dedicated consumer and in-store marketing experts.

Roles/Capabilities—Summary and Implications

The Mission informs the ideal organization and helps identify the required roles.

The Vision helps identify which roles are required to be best in class.

Match performance, strengths, motivation, and fit of individuals and roles.

- Support and develop high performers in right roles.
- Help improve performance of low performers in right roles.

- Evolve high performers in wrong roles to better roles over time.
- Move low performers in wrong roles to better roles now.

Structure flows out of organization's mission and strategy.

Think through operational, informational, and financial structures.

Provide structure that is necessary and sufficient only.

Some of your most painful choices are going to be in this area. This is one of those areas where trying to please everybody will lead to pleasing nobody. Choosing to act on people who are in the wrong roles is generally not the most enjoyable part of leadership. But it is an essential part.

QUESTIONS YOU SHOULD ASK YOURSELF

- Am I moving at the right speed to get the right people in the right roles?
- Do I have appropriate back up and contingency plans?

Downloadable TOOL 10.1
Performance/Potential Grid*

Performance
(Results, Behaviors, and Communication)

| | Below Standard | Standard | Above Standard |

	Below Standard	Above Standard
Right Role	Help improve performance soon	Support and develop
Okay Role		
Wrong Role	Move to better role now	Evolve to better role over time

Potential
(Strengths, Motivation, and Fit)

People Actions

Right role/above standard: Keep in current roles. Support and develop them. These people are helping and will continue to help. Make sure to push their compensation, employability, meaning in the work, and share in shaping the destiny as high as possible.

Right role/below standard: Invest to improve these people's performance. They can deliver with the right direction, training, and support.

Wrong role/above standard: Actively look for better fit before performance drops. Resist the temptation to keep in current role. They are helping, but the potential exists for even more.

Wrong role/below standard: Move to a better role inside or outside the team—immediately.

Shape the Team *Culture* with an Ongoing Communication Campaign (throughout Your First 100 Days)

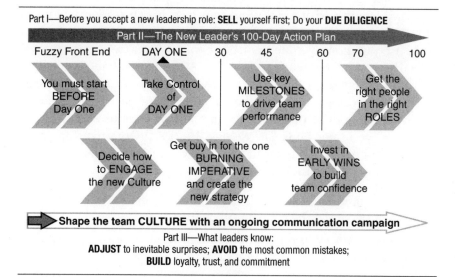

Part I—Before you accept a new leadership role: **SELL** yourself first; Do your **DUE DILIGENCE**

Part II—The New Leader's 100-Day Action Plan

| Fuzzy Front End | DAY ONE | 30 | 45 | 60 | 70 | 100 |

You must start BEFORE Day One

Take Control of DAY ONE

Use key MILESTONES to drive team performance

Get the right people in the right ROLES

Decide how to ENGAGE the new Culture

Get buy in for the one BURNING IMPERATIVE and create the new strategy

Invest in EARLY WINS to build team confidence

Shape the team CULTURE with an ongoing communication campaign

Part III—What leaders know:
ADJUST to inevitable surprises; **AVOID** the most common mistakes;
BUILD loyalty, trust, and commitment

Culture is a combination of people and practices—habits. By culture, we have in mind what happens when the burning imperative gels into a dynamic and live organizational mind-set. It is the hardest and most lengthy part of a comprehensive business change, it cannot be created overnight and will never happen if the foundations are not carefully laid and challenges to the mission are not appropriately handled. You have to map the existing culture and the coalitions. Then you have to engage in an all-out, multimedia campaign over an extended period to shape the culture to where it needs to be. Doing this right requires a lot of effort. The payoff is huge.

To paraphrase Aristotle; Excellence is an art won by training and habituation. We do not act right because we have virtue or excellence, but we rather have those because we have acted right. We are what we repeatedly do. Excellence, then, is not an act but a habit. These habits can help or hurt transitions.

For example, culture can be a barrier when the CEO's power is undercut by passive aggressive handling of conflict within the organization. A couple of years ago, Coca-Cola's CEO directed a change in the positioning statement of a brand that was marketed in Japan only. Later, someone asked the Japanese brand team for a translation of the new positioning. What they gave him was identical to the old positioning. When he challenged them, they explained that there were two positioning statements: one for "Atlanta" and one that was actually used in the market. Only the "Atlanta" one had changed.

Until changes become part of the ongoing culture of the firm, until they become habit, the change effort is not complete. Jeannie Daniel Duck does a nice job of laying out the various stages of cultural change in her book *The Change Monster*.[1] Organizations must move through several stages of a change curve to really embed a cultural change. Those include:

- *Stagnation:* During which the organization is depressed or hyperactive until the decision to change is made.
- *Preparation:* Planning and communication until appetite for change reaches critical mass.
- *Implementation:* Sharing vision, strategy, and plans, initiatives in place leading up to real awareness that something is wrong.
- *Determination:* Conflicts, clashes, failures, and minor successes lead up to a moment of crisis after which change is abandoned or results are realized.
- *Fruition:* Before more change is required.

One of Jeannie's key warnings is that leadership teams often mistake Implementation for Fruition. Just because the leadership team has started making changes does not mean the entire organization has embraced them. And it certainly doesn't mean everyone in the organization has made the changes into a habit.

---

[1] Jeannie Daniel Duck, *The Change Monster*, New York: Three Rivers Press, 2001.

Changing a culture is a huge task. The more people and complexity there is in a business, the harder it is. Change always involves changing the attitudes and behaviors of people as individuals. And it will be easier and more effective if it flows out of a new or renewed imperative—especially the imperative's values.

Communication—Shaping the Team Culture

If building tactical capacity is all about aligning people, plans, and practices around a burning imperative, an internal communication campaign is the key aligning tool you'll deploy in conjunction with getting milestones in place, early wins tied up, roles sorted, and reinforcement of the culture or "habits" that you are trying to shape.

Coming out of the burning imperative session, you have a picture of:

- The case for change
- A compelling vision
- Achievable next steps

Once those elements are in place, a carefully crafted communication plan is essential to making them come alive. Critical components of the campaign are going to include:

- An overarching message
- Key communication points
- Signs and symbols, icons, heroes and devils
- Media choices
- Touch points over time

Ideally, you will pull these together to empower others on your core team to drive the burning imperative through their groups. The four-point method that follows is an efficient and comprehensive way of crafting and communicating the teams burning imperative to all that need to know. Follow these steps and your communication plan will become your strong ally in shaping the team culture:

1. *Transparent milestones*, publicly set, tracked, and adjusted as appropriate
2. *Early wins* that you will over-invest in to deliver and celebrate as examples for others
3. *Reinvigorating* the campaign during the inevitable crisis of confidence

FIGURE 11.1 Shaping Team Culture

Prep	Case for change x Compelling vision x Doable next steps
	Message, Communication Points, Signs and Symbols, Media, Touch Points

Launch Campaign	Cascade Milestones	Celebrate Early Wins	Reinforce	Institutionalize
Kick off Roll out Deep dive	Public scorecard Track and report Adjust	Over-invest Deliver Publicize	Early warning system Adjustments Recommitment	Recognition and reward Practices and systems Control points

4. *Institutionalizing* the change with supporting practices at the right time

Figure 11.1 shows how it all looks.

Prep

To prepare, you have to get the tools in place:

- Finalizing the overarching message
- Determining the key communication points
- Choosing the signs and symbols to leverage
- Laying out your internal media plan
- Mapping out the touch points

Message

Great communication campaigns pivot off of a central message. Think "It's the economy stupid!" for Clinton's campaign. Think "Morning in America" for Reagan's campaign. Or a "Ford in every driveway." Or "We're going to be #1 or #2 or we're going to get out" for one of Jack Welch's early drives at GE. The point is, you need an overriding message to anchor the campaign. A good place to look for it is in the compelling vision of the future that came out of your imperative workshop.

Communication Points

Next come the key communication points. In most cases, it is most effective just to let these fall out of the:

- Case for change (with key points following that)
- Compelling vision of the future (with key points)
- Doable next steps (with key points)

Signs and Symbols, Icons, Heroes and Devils

Often, signs and symbols can speak louder than words. Some of the most compelling are how you spend your time changing control point metrics and processes; changing the way decisions are made; changing communication norms around mode, manner, or frequency, recognizing evidence of changes in behaviors and attitudes; celebrating early wins; making appropriate role changes; acquiring or divesting companies, divisions, services, functions, talent; and publicly hanging those that won't make the change (figuratively speaking, of course).

Coca-Cola's team in the United Kingdom had been told for years all the things they could not do. The company's managers had been very defensive about their market leadership position and did not want to do anything to hasten its erosion. Additionally, Coca-Cola and its bottling partner were continually battling over the right way to do things and allocate marketing spending and profits. John was looking for a way to send a message that things were going to change. His opportunity came when the United Kingdom changed its national laws to allow the trademarking of a shape. Coca-Cola got awarded the first ever trademark on a shape for its well-known contour bottle.

John jumped on the opportunity and assembled the Coca-Cola brand team, two competing advertising agencies, and two competing public relations agencies. He opened the meeting by saying:

The stars have aligned. We have the strongest brand, the best team and now, the first-ever shape trademark for our contour bottle. I would like you to show me a plan to get 100 percent awareness of our new trademark within 24 hours of announcing it. I have more money to spend than you have ideas so here is the deal. I will come back in eight hours to see your plan. I will approve or disapprove your plan on the spot. If I go through the elements of the plan and say "Yes. Yes. Yes. Yes. Yes." to all the elements, you will have failed. Because, unless you can come up with an idea that I do not have the guts to approve on the spot, you will not have pushed hard enough. See you at five o'clock.

And he walked out.

At five o'clock, the team presented a plan to put a cold contour bottle of Coca-Cola in the hands of every consumer in the United Kingdom on one day. Two million bottles would be handed out. Everyone else would be given a coupon for a free bottle, good that day only. The whole thing would be supported by a massive advertising and public relations effort.

John asked some questions along the way and when the presentation was done said only "Go do it."

Stanley, the marketing director of Coca-Cola who had led the presentation said, "What do you mean?"

John: "I only said three words. Which one don't you understand?"

Stanley: "Do you want us to write up a proposal?"

John: "No. I want you to execute your plan."

Stanley: "Do you want us to share it with the group president?"

John: "No. I'm approving your plan. Go do it."

Stanley: "But this could cost $3MM+."

John: "I'm authorizing you to spend the money."

Stanley: "Wait a minute. We have only been working on this for a couple of hours. I've got a lot of unanswered questions."

John: "Stanley, you're the director of marketing for Coca-Cola. You should have questions. Go get answers to your questions. And when you're satisfied with the answers, modify your plan and then put it in the market. But don't come back and talk to me about it any more."

And they did. And it doubled the brand's growth rate.

Learning: John used this opportunity to make a huge symbolic gesture to sow seeds of a new culture of making faster decisions and taking risks to accelerate growth.

Media

There is a whole range of ways to deliver messages to different groups. It might be helpful to think in terms of a matrix (on p. 155).

	Individual (One-on-One)	Small Group	Large Group
Face-to-face			
Phone			
Video conference			
Voicemail	(Deploy with different groups)		
Handwritten notes	(At different times)		
Typed notes			
E-mail			
Mass communication (events, bulletin boards, intranet, chat, pop-ups, etc.)			

Touch Points

The media plan needs to include touch points over time. This is not a one-time event. An effective communication campaign must include multiple touch points in multiple venues. Think in terms of Gross Rating Points (GRPs), defined by the number of people you reach times the frequency of touch. These fall out of the media plan. For key individuals and groups, map out a series of touch points including face-to-face conversations, phone calls, video conferences, notes, e-mails, and more general mass communication.

Once you have these thought through, you are ready to implement.

Launch

Do not be afraid of a big launch. The way you launch the campaign could be one of the signs and symbols. Look at the presidential party conventions. For the most part, they are shows. But they know that everything communicates and they are very careful about who speaks, when, saying what against what backdrop. You should do no less.

You will likely want to kick off the campaign and follow that up with some sort of broader roll out—either through subgroup meetings or mass communication. You might, for example, do something like this:

- Follow up meetings or phone calls with each individual who was at the Burning Imperative workshop.
- Subteam workshops/meetings to gain buy-in to the burning imperative.
- Regrouping with the core team to gather input and adjust as appropriate and practical.
- "All-hands" meeting, video or call to launch the final burning imperative and plan.
- Follow-up "all-hands" note confirming the burning imperative.
- Follow-up phone calls with each individual on core team after the "all-hands" meeting.
- Deep dive with selected individuals to drive the message.

Cascade Milestones

However, you choose to do it, launching is a major step. But you've just begun. Now you have to make it real by proving that you are going to drive those achievable next steps. This is where you will likely want to deploy some sort of public scorecard where everyone can see results against key milestones.

Make sure you are clear on what you are going to track. Make sure you actually do track it and report it. And make sure you're driving your key communication points at every touch point having to do with milestones—with your core team, their direct reports, and deep-dive meetings throughout the organization. Then, adjust what is going on to drive the milestones that are on track even faster and get caught up on the ones that are falling behind.

Repeating the Message

In this effort, repetition is not just good, it's essential. Let me say it again—repetition is not just good, it's essential. In other words, you're going to have to create different ways and times to repeat the same message over and over again with what you say and what you do. You'll get bored with your own message well before the critical mass has internalized it. So, don't shy away from repeating it. And when you're done, do it again. Because, just in case you didn't get the point, in this effort, repetition is not just good, it's essential.

Celebrate Early Wins

Somewhere along the way, you identified a dramatic early win for your first six months. As part of this campaign, you will have over-invested to deliver that win. When it is complete, celebrate it. And celebrate it publicly. This is all about giving the team confidence in itself. So invest your time to make the team members feel great.

Reinforce

There is going to be a crisis of confidence at some point. At that point, the team will question whether you're really serious about these changes and whether the changes you are making are going to stick. Be ready for the crisis and use that moment to reinforce your efforts.

The first thing you have to do is to have an early warning system in place to see the crisis developing. Think in terms of eyes and ears throughout the organization. These are going to be people who feel safe telling you what's really going on. They might be administrative staff. They might be people outside your direct line of reports. Or they might be people far enough removed from you that they don't feel threatened telling you the truth. Whoever they are, you need to identify them and cultivate them.

The main sign of the impending crisis will be the nay-sayers or detractors raising their heads and their objections again. It is likely they will go quiet during the period of initial enthusiasm after the launch of the burning imperative. But they'll find it impossible to stay quiet forever. Their coming back will be the first signs of the crisis.

And their point of view will spread if you don't cut it off.

So hit the restart button fast. Make it clear that you are committed to the changes. Regroup your core team to confirm their commitment. Take action against the blocking coalitions. This is a good time to publicly shine the spotlight on some people who are still in the way. Some good steps at this point include:

- Regroup with core team to gather input and adjust as appropriate.
- "All-hands" meeting, video or call to highlight progress and reinforce the burning imperative.

- Follow-up note confirming commitment imperative.
- Follow-up phone calls with each individual on core team.
- Reinforce imperative at each key milestone with core team, their teams, and others.
- Skip level meetings.
- Skip level one-on-ones and field/plant visits.
- Continuously monitor.

Institutionalizing the Change

Coming out of the crisis is a good time to start institutionalizing the changes. You cannot spend a lot of time waiting for the next crisis and you will need to move on to the next set of changes. So, you'll want to put in place practices that will ensure the changes you made so far become part of the core fabric of how you do business.

A good place to start is with the recognition and reward systems. Make sure they are modified to recognize the behaviors and attitudes that are important in the new way of doing business. Make sure they reward the results you want and do not reward the results you do not want.

Other ripe areas for systemic changes are the whole communication, decision, and control point triumvirate. Modify the modes, manner, and frequency of communication to fit the new state. Modify how decisions are made, pushing them as close to the customer as you can. Modify control points so you are measuring the right thing with the right reporting processes.

A third area to pay close attention to is the talent acquisition, development, and succession planning process. Make sure you are recruiting people who will support the new direction and values. Make sure you are building the new direction and values into your development plans. And make sure you're moving the right people through the system. Promotions can be a very powerful sign and symbol of what you value.

Beyond these three, there is a whole host of other supporting systems and practices that you can line up to reinforce the new way of doing business.

One of these can be as simple as basic geography. When *Le Monde*, the leading daily newspaper in Paris, decided to invest heavily in a web-based edition of the daily newspaper, it realized that everything about this new medium, starting with the age of the people who were comfortable and proficient in its basic technology, was different than the core business. The senior leadership made a bold and brave decision. They decided to set up an entirely separate affiliate and physically place the offices on the other side of Paris. They knew that some day the fragile young chick would be strong enough to handle the fierce competition for resources and influence that is the basic culture of the newspaper. To start with, the offshoot needed to go through its own awkward age without being crushed by its stronger siblings.

Culture change management Tool 11.1 on page 161 provides a good framework for thinking about creating cultural change. At any moment, there will be people helping to move the organization toward the new culture and people hindering your progress. A key point is that the same people may be doing different things at different times. So it's important to update the "map" regularly and keep driving the change with implementation of the communication and change plan.

HOT TIP

Think in Terms of a Communication Campaign: Craft your core message and key communication points and drive them over, and over, and over throughout the organization. Shaping the culture is hard work. But it will be one of the most important and most enduring things you do.

The Case of the Filtered Vision

Pollio, a cheese producer on the East Coast, had recently hired a new CEO. As he came to work in his first week, he noticed several Cadillacs in the parking lot and asked who owned them. He was interested to learn they belonged to the cheese company's route drivers. The route drivers were the heart and soul of the company. They were the ones who sold and serviced the company's mainstay deli customers. Each of them "owned" their route and had for years. While the new CEO certainly wanted them to be fairly compensated for their contributions, he did not understand how they could all afford Cadillacs.

So he mapped out a typical driver's day:

- Load truck with cheese.
- Sell cheese to accounts.
- Deliver cheese to store from supplies on truck.

- Collect payment.
- Return unsold cheese to depot and turn in receipts.

The issues were that:

- No one kept track of how much cheese was put on the trucks.
- There were no price lists.
- All sales were cash.
- No one counted how much cheese was returned to the depot.

This was the way things had always operated. The company had been profitable. The drivers had been loyal. No one wanted to "rock the boat." So everyone convinced themselves that things were fine and continued viewing the world through their self-imposed filters. Needless to say, the new CEO made substantial changes to this system on fast timing.

Culture/Communication—Summary and Implications

Culture is combination of people and practices—the behavior and attitudes behind what people actually do. It is usually the most difficult and most lengthy part of a comprehensive business change.

Begin with the end, keep the new culture in mind and then map out how to change the attitudes and behaviors of all (contributors, detractors, and watchers) required to get there.

The communication campaign's key components include:

- Launching the campaign, pivoting off key message and communication points
- Cascading milestones throughout the organization
- Celebrating the early wins that reinforce the new direction
- Reinforcing the campaign as needed
- Institutionalizing the change by changing key practices

QUESTIONS YOU SHOULD ASK YOURSELF

- Is the message compelling?
- Is the campaign strong enough to drive the imperative?

Downloadable TOOL 11.1
Communication
Campaign Milestones*

	How	Who	When

Plan Ready

• Message/communication points _____

• Signs and symbols identified _____

• Media and touch points set _____

Launch Campaign

• Kick off _____

• Roll out _____

• Deep dive _____

Cascade Milestones

• Public scorecard _____

• Track and report _____

• Adjust _____

Reinforce

• Early warnings _____

• Adjustments _____

• Recommit _____

Institutionalize

• Recognition and reward _____

• Practices _____

• Control points _____

Downloadable TOOL 11.2
Culture Change Management*

Key Steps

1. Identify "new" **desired culture** you are trying to create.

_____

_____

2. Evaluate **current culture** (behaviors, attitudes, contributors, detractors).

_____

_____

3. Detail what changes need to be made to move from current to new:

   • Consider the impact of shifts.

_____

_____

   • Key considerations/changes.

_____

_____

4. Create communication and change plan:

   • Change map of key stakeholders.

_____

_____

Downloadable TOOL 11.2 (Continued)

- Identify key individuals' roles in change (block it, watch it, help it, make it happen).

\
\

- Determine effective ways to move stakeholders to appropriate level of support.

\
\

- Develop and implement a detailed communication plan.

\
\

5. Test progress at checkpoints along the way.

Downloadable TOOL 11.3
Communication Planning*

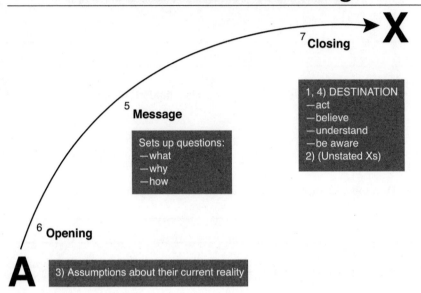

1. Identify destination:

   • What is the desired reaction and behavior you want from you audience/
   constituents?

   _____

   _____

   • What specifically do you want, not want them to understand, believe, say
   about you, do?

   _____

   _____

2. Be explicit about unstated Xs. What you want listener to think about you?

   _____

   _____

   _____

Downloadable TOOL 11.3 (Continued)

3. Assess current reality:

   • What does your audience/constituents currently understand, believe, say about you? Why?

   _____

   _____

   • Develop a risk management plan including: potential obstacles, negative rumors, sabotage, legal requirements, unintended consequences, scenarios.

   _____

   _____

4. Reevaluate destination in light of assumptions about audience.

   _____

   _____

5. Bridge the gap:

   • What do they need to be aware of, understand, and believe to move from current reality to your destination?

   _____

   _____

Develop core messages and key communication points:

   • Limit core messages to five at the maximum.

   _____

   _____

6. Package the message:

   • How should core messages be packaged for optimum effectiveness?

   _____

   _____

   _____

(continued)

Downloadable TOOL 11.3   (Continued)

- What kind of supporting data do you need?

_____

_____

- What is your key opening message?

_____

_____

- What is your key closing message?

_____

_____

7. Deliver the message:

- What are the best vehicles to reach your audience or constituents? What is optimum combination? What is the best timing to release the message? Who and what influences whom?

_____

_____

- How do you best plant the follow-up seeds?

_____

_____

WHAT LEADERS KNOW

CHAPTER 12

Adjust to the Inevitable Surprises

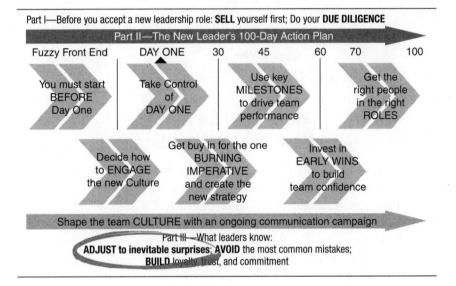

Part I—Before you accept a new leadership role: **SELL** yourself first; Do your **DUE DILIGENCE**

Part II—The New Leader's 100-Day Action Plan

| Fuzzy Front End | DAY ONE | 30 | 45 | 60 | 70 | 100 |

You must start
BEFORE
Day One

Take Control
of
DAY ONE

Use key
MILESTONES
to drive team
performance

Get the
right people
in the right
ROLES

Decide how
to ENGAGE
the new Culture

Get buy in for the one
BURNING
IMPERATIVE
and create the
new strategy

Invest in
EARLY WINS
to build
team confidence

Shape the team CULTURE with an ongoing communication campaign

Part III—What leaders know:
ADJUST to inevitable surprises; AVOID the most common mistakes;
BUILD loyalty, trust, and commitment

Nothing endures but change has been a constant refrain from Heraclitus to Darwin to Toffler. One of the main advantages to starting early and deploying the building blocks of Tactical Capacity quickly is that you and your team will be ready that much sooner to adjust to changing circumstances and surprises. Remember, the ability to respond flexibly and fluidly is one of the hallmarks of a team with Tactical Capacity. Don't fight change. Find the upside opportunities it creates.

Not all surprises are equal. Job one is to sort them out to guide your own and your team's response. If it's a temporary, minor blip, keep your team focused on its existing priorities. If it's minor, but enduring, factor it into your ongoing team evolution. Major surprises are a different game. If they're enduring, you'll need to react and make some fundamental changes to deal with the new reality. If they're temporary, you'll want to move into crisis or incident management as we've laid out later in the chapter.

	Enduring Impact	**Temporary Impact**
Major	Fundamental redeployment	Crisis or incident management
Minor	Factor into ongoing team evolution	Downplay and stay focused on priorities

Major and Enduring: New Responsibilities

If you follow the methodology laid out in this book, do not be surprised to find the organization asking you to take on increased responsibility before you think you are ready. Of course, having read this book, you will be ready.

For situations like that, our advice is one word: *RESTART.*

Go right back to the beginning. It is a new role with its own set of opportunities and risks. Go right back to due diligence and make sure you understand the organization, role, and personal risk. Internal transfers or promotions or responsibility add-ons have an added element of challenge because it is often hard to say no. Your world changes the minute the organization asks you to change. You cannot go back to the way things were before they offered you the change.

Thus, your due diligence may not be as thorough as you can do coming into a new company. However, as an insider, you should know more to start with.

The *organization risk* is different as an insider. It's harder to walk away from the overall organization. If the part of the overall organization you've been asked to move into is in trouble, you may have to figure out a way to turn it around. Still, you want to understand the organization's sustainable competitive advantage.

The *role risk* is the same. You have to make sure key stakeholders are aligned around the role. Find out who had concerns about the way the role was designed. Find out what was done to make them feel better about it now. One thing you can do as an insider that might have been harder as an outsider coming in is to talk to the people that were concerned directly.

The *personal risk* should be less. Because you are there, the organization knows you. So it's less likely you will have been able to convince them that you have strengths that you don't have. Still, it is worth asking what, specifically, about you led them to offering you the job.

Having completed some sort of due diligence, you need to build in as much of a fuzzy front end as possible. Recall that the key steps for the fuzzy front end include:

- Identify *key* stakeholders Up, Across, and Down.
- Manage personal set-up (particularly office changes here).
- Conduct prestart meetings and phone calls (essential).
- Gather prestart information and learning (some you'll have).
- Plan your first 100 days (worth the investment of time).

We already shared with you the example of Harold who was 100 days into his role as vice president of marketing when his boss asked him to pick up business development as well. His restart was clean because the organizations were separate. So he kept marketing chugging along as it had and did a new 100-day restart with the business development group.

It is trickier when the groups are merging. It is tempting just to fold the new group into the existing group. Although tempting, it is generally not optimal. Just as you want to make the best possible start in a new role, people coming to work for you want to make the best possible start in their new roles. And even if they're doing the same thing, if they're merging into your group, it's a new role. Net, when groups merge, it is generally best to go right back to the beginning with everyone and move into major redeployment mode.

Quarterly Updates

You would hope that once you get these building blocks in place, the team would run smoothly. And it might, if nothing changes. Not adjusting to change is often the hidden landmine that derails leaders and their teams. We have talked about the need to adjust to major changes—both crises with potential negative impact and opportunities with potential positive impact. The team will also need to adjust to the neverending series of minor changes.

For these, you will likely want to put in place quarterly updates. Some leaders take a couple of days out each quarter for their core team to stop and think. Some leaders make it a day or less. However you decide to do it, you should build in some sort of regular check to make sure you're not missing an accumulation of minor changes.

Major, But Temporary: Events and Crises

Major events are good things. Crises are bad things. Just as a crisis handled well can turn into a good thing, a major event handled poorly can easily turn into a very bad crisis. The difference comes down to planning, implementation, and follow through; and mostly planning. To help with these, we've included some ideas on crisis or incident management and then a little more detail on communicating in a crisis or incident. They're in the form of a checklist (Tools 12.1 on p. 173 and 12.2 on p. 180) so they are immediately actionable.

Adjust to the Inevitable Surprises—
Summary and Implications

Monitoring the situation is not an optional exercise. You must be ready for internal and external changes, incidents, crises, and opportunities.

Be ready for organizational or situational changes that require you to restart—things like new bosses, new competitors, mergers, promotions, and the like. In these situations, go back and reassess the organizational, role, and personal risks and build new relationships as appropriate.

Be ready for crises and incidents. For them, follow the basic flow of prepare—understand—plan—implement—revise/prepare. Make sure to manage communication in and out throughout the situation.

Downloadable TOOL 12.1
Crisis Management Checklist*

In almost any crisis management situation, you should follow the basic flow of:

Prepare—Understand—Plan—Implement—Revise/Prepare.

Prepare

Have an incident/crisis management team and process in place and ready to go in advance.

In place? _____ Team leader: _____

Then, once the incident hits:

Understand

Pause for a moment to figure out what you know and think:

• What do we know for a fact?

_____

_____

• What do we not know, but need to know?

_____

_____

• What do we think/conclude is going on?

_____

_____

• What do we predict may happen (scenarios)?

_____

_____

• What are the potential issues and risks?

_____

_____

(continued)

Downloadable TOOL 12.1 (Continued)

Do a quick SWOT analysis (strengths, weaknesses, opportunities, threats).

• What are our assets?

_____

_____

• Gaps?

_____

_____

• Situational things we can take advantage of?

_____

_____

• Risks?

_____

_____

Plan

• What want to happen (under the different scenarios)?

_____

_____

• What do to make that happen (under different scenarios)?

—Immediate actions to fix problem

_____

_____

—Longer-term actions to prevent recurrence

_____

_____

_____

Downloadable TOOL 12.1 (Continued)

- What will we communicate to all our constituents (consumer, customer, management, employees, media, health authorities, etc.)?

  —In what order will we communicate to them?

  _____

  _____

  —Will our communication be proactive or reactive?

  _____

  _____

- Identify single crisis manager: _____
- Identify single spokesperson: _____
- Clarify exactly what you are doing with what resources and when you are doing it.

  _____

  _____

Implement

- Move quickly and decisively to contain and control incident:

  —Isolate the situation: contain; prevent spreading; limit entry, preventing extraneous people and factors from interfering and complicating the situation.

  —Deal with injuries.

  —Stabilize the situation: stop momentum. (Take no actions that exacerbates the situation or creates new problems such as placing blame, inflammatory comments, or ignoring opinions and recommendations of others.)

- Provide frequent updates as information gaps are filled:

  —Assemble and evaluate accuracy of available information.

  _____

  _____

  —Notify and update community contacts (police, fire, etc.).

  _____

  _____

(continued)

Downloadable TOOL 12.1   (Continued)

—Set up operations and communications centers.

_____

_____

—Delegate responsibility for functional support/response teams and communication.

_____

_____

• Monitor and track the situation, progress, and response and adjust as needed:

—Ensure stability.

—Reconfirm accuracy of information and keep communication channels open.

—Offer trauma counseling.

—Continue to liaison with authorities.

—Keep all promises made.

• Over-communicate across the team every step of the way.

Then, when crisis/incident is over:

• Thank authorities and contributors.

Revise/Prepare

General Debrief

• When were we aware of the incident/event?

_____

_____

• What signals were recognized, not recognized?

_____

_____

• When did we first sense a problem?

_____

_____

_____

Downloadable TOOL 12.1   (Continued)

- When did it become a crisis?

_____

_____

- What caused the crisis?

_____

_____

- What was considered in prior vulnerability inventory?

_____

_____

- Did we accurately assess impact of problem?

_____

_____

- Have we ever rehearsed for this?

_____

_____

Debrief Planning

- Did we plan effectively? What improvements can we make?

_____

_____

- Were the necessary resources available (including medical, legal, PR, technical, management, and an effective notification system)?

_____

_____

- How effective was the written plan?

_____

_____

_____

(continued)

Downloadable TOOL 12.1　(Continued)

• Were our people knowledgeable about their roles and others' roles?

_____

_____

• Was there any undue confusion or conflict?

_____

_____

• Were sufficient personnel available with the mix right?

_____

_____

• Did we have adequate equipment, facilities, resources? Anything inadequate, need changes, need enhancements?

_____

_____

• How current was the information?

_____

_____

Debrief Success or Failure

• How quickly did we bring the crisis under control?

_____

_____

• How well did we work with government agencies?

_____

_____

• How well did we communicate with key audiences?

_____

_____

_____

Downloadable TOOL 12.1   (Continued)

- What was the public's view of our actions?

_____

_____

- What was the view of other audiences?

_____

_____

- What is our own view of our actions? Did we meet our own objectives?

_____

_____

- How well did we preserve our credibility?

_____

_____

- What steps can we take now to ensure continued productive company operations?

_____

_____

_____

- Lessons/trends to share with others: What did we do particularly well that should be continued and cascaded? What needs to be improved?

_____

_____

_____

Modify policies and practices as appropriate.

Downloadable TOOL 12.2
Crisis Communication Checklist*

Communication Preparation

• Anticipate questions.

_____

_____

• Know each audience and their interest factors (competition, conflict, contro-
versy, consequences, familiar person, heartstrings, humor, problem, progress, success, unknown, unusual, wants/needs). Your SWOT analysis will
answer some of these questions.

_____

_____

Communication Approach

There are usually many ways in which you can communicate and many possible messages to convey. There are many choices and often they need to be
made quickly. Before going forward, you'll need to decide:

• What method of communication is the best to achieve our objective?

_____

_____

• What key messages do we want to drive?

_____

_____

There should never be more than three.

Make everyone who is in a position to communicate aware of the key messages. Insist that they focus on them. Consider questions as merely cues to
drive home the key messages. Time and control remains on your side if you
stay focused on controlling the dialogue by focusing on the key messages. If
you move beyond the key messages, the other side will assume control of the
dialogue which is usually not advantageous to your communication objectives.

Downloadable TOOL 12.2   (Continued)

- How can you support you key messages? You can find support in facts, personal experience, contrasts, comparisons, analogies, expert opinion, analysis, definition, statistics, and examples.

_____

_____

_____

_____

Once you have your method of communication, your key messages, and your support, you can then move into implementation.

Communication Implementation

1. Show concern (especially if there's a crisis).

2. Communicate quickly (no indecision).

3. Communicate credibly (tell the truth; release only confirmed facts; correct significant errors and counteract negatives; stay calm).

4. Communicate thoroughly (proactively release updates).

After the incident, communication does not stop. Be prepared to revise and prepare for the next communication attempt. In some crises of great magnitude or high interest, there may be several cycles of communication stretching over long periods. Or it may just be one communication event, but most likely there will be others to follow at some point in the future. Therefore, this last and final step is essential.

CHAPTER 13

Avoid the Most Common Mistakes

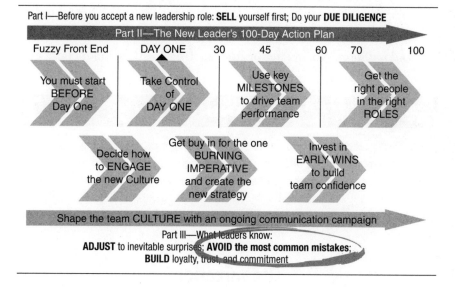

Part I—Before you accept a new leadership role: **SELL** yourself first; Do your **DUE DILIGENCE**

Part II—The New Leader's 100-Day Action Plan

Fuzzy Front End   DAY ONE   30   45   60   70   100

You must start BEFORE Day One

Take Control of DAY ONE

Use key MILESTONES to drive team performance

Get the right people in the right ROLES

Decide how to ENGAGE the new Culture

Get buy in for the one BURNING IMPERATIVE and create the new strategy

Invest in EARLY WINS to build team confidence

Shape the team CULTURE with an ongoing communication campaign

Part III—What leaders know:
ADJUST to inevitable surprises; **AVOID the most common mistakes**; **BUILD** loyalty, trust, and commitment

We keep alluding to the risks of on-boarding. You cannot reduce the risks inherent in a new role until you understand them. Of the seven major on-boarding risks, three need to be assessed during the due diligence stage of on-boarding: *organization*, *role*, and *personal* risks. Then, two can be jumpstarted during the fuzzy front end: *relationships* and *learning*. *Delivery* risk needs to be tackled during your first 100 days. And *adjustment* risk needs to be dealt with as appropriate. By way of review, the seven risks of on-boarding are listed here:

The Seven Risks of On-Boarding

1. *Organization:* Lack of a winning strategy or inability to implement that strategy
2. *Role:* Expectations and resources or key stakeholders not aligned
3. *Personal:* Gaps in individual's strengths, motivation, or fit
4. *Relationship:* Failing to establish/maintain key relationships Up, Across, or Down
5. *Learning:* Less than adequate understanding of the situation, customers, collaborators, capabilities, competitors, or conditions
6. *Delivery:* Failing to build a high-performing team and to deliver results fast enough
7. *Adjustment:* Not seeing or not reacting to situational changes

WARNING!

We are going to describe these risks one by one. But they frequently come in multiples and often interact with each other. Exposure to one risk heightens other risks, and failure has a way of gaining its own terrible and often unstoppable momentum.

Organization

This risk is that the organization will fail no matter what you do. Mitigating this risk is about making sure you do not get on board a ship that is already sunk. Certainly, some people will go into organizations knowing this risk is high. Some people thrive on this risk and want to be part of the turnaround. Vince Lombardi took on that risk as a young coach with the failing Green Bay Packers. Then he did it again with the failing Red Skins. That is great stuff. That is a powerful choice. It is important to make sure that it is a choice, that you know what you're getting into and that you are not joining an organization that's in trouble without knowing it.

In general, the issue seems to be either that the organization does not have a winning strategy or that it is unable to implement that strategy.

Role

Just as important as negotiating the package, if not more important, is negotiating roles and responsibilities, expectations, and resources. To figure out exactly how things are going to work, far more is required than the job specifications and the discussions that have occurred up to this point.

The critical piece is what new leaders' bosses expect them to deliver and what resources they can control and influence to make that happen. They must make sure they have the resources they need to deliver on their boss's expectations. And they must make sure the other key players are aligned around those deliverables and resource allocations.

Personal

Candidates should be selling during the "dance of the bumble bees." The danger of this is that sometimes candidates sell companies on hiring them even though the match between their strengths, motivation, fit, and what the company really needs is suboptimal. That is fine—just so long as candidates stop at this point and take a hard look at themselves. It is far less painful to turn down the wrong job than to try to succeed in it.

Relationship

This landmine catches many people. It is especially tricky because sometimes the results of stepping on it do not show up for months, or longer. What is worse, you can get caught by it through pure neglect.

Relationship risks are particularly severe for people who are brought in to be change agents. Often those people come in with a hero mentality, thinking they are the organization's savior. Thinking they are the savior is not always a problem because sometimes they're right. The problem is when new leaders act as if they are the savior. It is impossible to act like a savior and be a team leader at the same time. You have to choose one or the other. Always choose the latter. The world is littered with many dead heroes who never made it home:

"Zach. We've got to let you go."

"Why?"

"You haven't been able to rally the troops. They can't keep up with the pace of change."

"But you told me to move fast and change things."

"I know. I just did not know it was going to be this painful. A couple of key people have come to me and said either you go or they go. And we can't afford to lose them."

Being Right versus Building Relationships

John was brought in to create a new global communications group, cutting across several functions and divisions. John was brilliant, charming, and had been phenomenally successful. He knew it. And even though everyone else knew it, he insisted on telling it to them over and over again. As much as they valued his insights and ideas, they could not stand being with him and stopped inviting him to meetings. It is hard to manage communications if no one wants to communicate with you.

Skipping Key People

Sebastian came in to the organization to create a new ventures group. He mapped most of the key stakeholders and was building relationships with them. After a while, it became apparent that the head of a different division was undermining what he was trying to do with her team. He did not understand why, since he had never come into contact with her. It turned out she was upset that he had not seen her as important enough to establish a relationship with. She was upset not at what he had done or said, but because he had not said anything to her at all. Sebastian overlooked her when he built his key stakeholder list and it cost him dearly months later.

Relying Too Heavily on the Organization Chart

Julie had been in place two months when she discovered there was a person reporting to her on the other side of the world. The other person had not been on the organization chart and no one had mentioned him to Julie. By the time Julie found the person and called him, he was convinced he was about to be fired since no one had given him any direction or input in two months.

You also have to map the way things really happen in the organization. There is always, *always,* a shadow organization. And often, that shadow organization is how things really get communicated and happen. Robert Woodruff made the key decisions at Coca-Cola for decades after he had officially retired from the board. You would be surprised how many times the guy holed up in a back office, never going to meetings controls key resources. Find those people and find them early. Make sure you build strong relationships with them.

Doing Wrong Things Right

The opposite risk to under investing in the right relationships is investing too much in the wrong relationships. It is tricky because early on it is difficult to know with certainty which are the right relationships to cultivate. You will not know whom to trust. But you've got to figure it out quickly. Look for signs. Look for clues. Do a few skip-level meetings. It is amazing how much people know about their bosses and their bosses' motives. And it's amazing how much they will tell you if you ask.

"The Way We Did It at . . ."

People struggle in the first job out of "academy" companies like Procter & Gamble, American Express, and General Electric. Those companies have extremely strong cultures, ways of doing things, and standards for excellence—as all companies should.

One of the issues people out of these companies face is that they are used to support, resources, and teammates who always deliver. When they got numbers from finance, they were right. When manufacturing said something was going to be ready, it was. While they should expect colleagues to deliver, it does not always happen that way. This is hard for people to accept at first. This, in turn, makes them prone to comments like:

"At xxx, this never would have happened."

"At xxx, we did it this way."

"At xxx, . . ."

The leader's colleagues at their new organization will get sick of this quickly. Talking about the way you did things at your previous company implies that your head or heart is still there. Do not do it. Nobody cares.

Out with the Old

There is a natural tendency to blame your predecessor for all the ills you inherited. On the surface, it feels like a good strategy. They are gone, not there to defend themselves. And centralizing the blame in them gets everyone else off the hook. The problem is that "your" team used to be "their" team. They own a lot your predecessor's successes and failures. It is hard to blame your predecessor without implicating your team. They will not like it. And they won't like you. Obviously, this is especially true if your predecessor got promoted and is now your boss. In this case, you have to position everything you do as building on previous successes.

Difficult Peers

Dealing with difficult people is unfortunately part of the job. In many cases, the key is playing for a tie. If you play to lose and give in to difficult people, they may keep coming back for more. If you play to win, they may become even more difficult. So, just play for a tie and be ready to walk away from conversations that are going nowhere.

Learning

It is almost a truism that it is important to learn about an organization before you can be effective. The faster you can get up to speed the better. While you cannot learn everything, this landmine manifests itself in the areas you fail to learn about. Misjudge the situation—ouch. Do not learn enough about key customers—ouch. Misunderstand key collaborators' needs—ouch. Miss holes in the organization's capabilities—ouch. Overlook a rising competitor—ouch. Misread changing externalities—ouch.

Beware of Changes to the Game

Harold joined a company that was helping companies take advantage of favorable tax treatments for new technologies. He had done his homework well across the board. He liked the team. They liked him. He knew exactly how he could add value to the group and to its customers. What he had failed to learn about was that the government was about to change the law and take away the favorable tax treatments. So, a few months into the job, the company effectively got legislated out of business.

Perception Is Reality

Truly, learning is essential. And being perceived as wanting to learn is just as important. You have heard it before: "seek first to understand,"[1] "don't come in with the answer,"[2] "wisdom begins in wonder."[3] You hear it repeatedly in many different ways, because it is proven advice. Heed it. You need to learn and you need to be perceived as being hungry to learn. Part of this is about learning. Part of this is about relationships.

Delivery

If you get everything else right but fail to deliver, you'll be gone. If you deliver, the organization can tolerate many other faults. If you are a sole practitioner you can perhaps deliver through your own sheer effort. If you are leading a team, you cannot deliver if the team doesn't deliver. Thus, the main risk here is that of failing to build a high-performance team fast enough to deliver the expected results in the expected time.

To be clear, this is about real delivery. It is not about manipulating expectations to get the base low. It is not about picking the wrong battles. It is not even about the process to get there. It is about putting points on the board with real impact.

Adjustment

Things change. And you need to change when things change. Sometimes you can get away with minor adjustments.

---

[1] Stephen Covey, *The Seven Habits of Highly Effective People,* New York: Simon & Schuster, 1989.
[2] Michael Watkins, *The First 90 Days,* Boston: Harvard Business School Press, 2003.
[3] Attributed to Socrates by "Brainy Quotes" online services.

Sometimes a complete restart is required. The risk lies in not seeing the need to change or in being to slow to react to change when you do see it.

Indirect Impacts Can Directly Impact You

Tony was brought into the company by Victor. Things were going okay in their division, but better in their sister division. After Tony had been there five months, the company promoted the head of the other division, Wendy, to head up both divisions. So now Tony was reporting to Victor reporting to Wendy. Tony thought that this move represented no big change for him.

He was wrong.

The change was huge and created an equally big adjustment. Any change in structure requires a relook at what is going on, if not a complete restart. Tony did not do that. He kept soldiering on, assuming that Victor would make his case to Wendy.

Two months later, Victor and everyone he had brought in to work for him, including Tony, were fired.

Avoid the Most Common Mistakes— Summary and Implications

There are seven on-boarding risks: organization, role, personal, learning, relationship, delivery, and adjustment.

You need to manage your own on-boarding in steps, mitigating, jumpstarting, or managing risks as appropriate:

- *Offer to acceptance:* Do a real due diligence to mitigate organizational, role, and personal risks.
- *Acceptance to start:* Get a jumpstart on learning and relationships.
- *After the start:* Build a high-performing team to execute, deliver, and adjust.

First prize is mitigating the organization, role, and personal risks during due diligence and jumpstarting the relationship and learning risks before you start. But if you can't, if they rear their ugly heads again, just keep yours and hit the restart button.

Build Loyalty, Trust, and Commitment

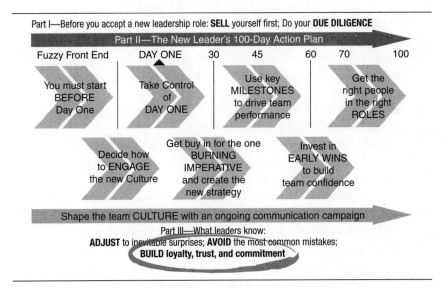

Part I—Before you accept a new leadership role: **SELL** yourself first; Do your **DUE DILIGENCE**

Part II—The New Leader's 100-Day Action Plan

| Fuzzy Front End | DAY ONE | 30 | 45 | 60 | 70 | 100 |

You must start **BEFORE** Day One

Take Control of **DAY ONE**

Use key **MILESTONES** to drive team performance

Get the right people in the right **ROLES**

Decide how to **ENGAGE** the new Culture

Get buy in for the one **BURNING IMPERATIVE** and create the new strategy

Invest in **EARLY WINS** to build team confidence

Shape the team **CULTURE** with an ongoing communication campaign

Part III—What leaders know:
ADJUST to inevitable surprises; **AVOID** the most common mistakes;
BUILD loyalty, trust, and commitment

T his book is about moving into new team leadership roles. Yet, we've buried our discussion about leadership in the final chapter on building loyalty, trust, and commitment. Why? Because great leaders think about their followers first. If you are reading this book, you are striving to be a better leader. You know that every chapter in this book so far is really about leadership. In this final chapter, we pull some of the loose ends together.

The key point of leverage for a complex transition is leadership. There are many visions of leadership. Ours is fundamentally anchored in the vision of building tactical capacity in a team. This capacity—this flexibility, energy, and skill—comes first from the leader. Your goal as a leader is to build it in each and every one of their team members. This kind of leadership is far from intuitive, and the lack of it, in the end, is a fatal stumbling block for many leaders of new ventures. The entire process needs to be driven by an awareness of the kind of leadership that ensures success in the challenging circumstances of a transition.

In the game "Follow the Leader," one child leads the others up, down, and around. The other children follow the leader just as long as the leader is going fun places, is a fun person, makes it fun for the other children, and knows what they are doing.

Leadership is just that simple—and just that complex. The leader is not necessarily the tallest, the oldest, the best dressed. And it's most definitely not necessarily the one with the grandest title. The best way to tell who's leading at any given moment is to see who the other kids are following.

A leader is the one the others follow. In business, like in the follow-the-leader game, people may follow different leaders at different times. Leaders may be better suited for some occasions than they are for others. Often leaders and followers trade places. And that's okay. The person who knows every branch of a tree should lead the climbing part and the person who knows every rock in the pond should lead the swimming part.

If you buy that, when you are looking to identify and understand the leader, you will look at the followers first. Why do people follow leaders? Because they:

- Want to go where the leader is going (fun places)
- Feel good about the leader as a person (fun person)
- Believe the leader has their best interests at heart (fun for the other kids)
- Trust the leader's judgment (knows what they are doing)

Where the leader is going: Generally, people will not follow other people to a place that they really do not want to go. Of course, there have been some stunning exceptions to this and there has been a whole lot written about the psychological background of seemingly irrational choices. But, for the most part, people will choose to go to fun places over "the valley of death." And the leader charging off in the wrong direction runs a huge risk of turning around and finding no one following—particularly in a complex transition.

This is why getting true buy-in to the burning imperative is so important. This is why it is not enough for a leader just to have a vision, but critically important for the leader's followers to buy into the mission and the vision. People will only follow toward a place, a vision that they care about. It is not about the leader. It is about the followers.

The leader as a person: Of course, it is about the leader as well. People need to feel good about the people with which they are associating. People hunt in pairs. Whether they treat their pair as a business partner or just a companion on the way, the choice of whom to hunt with is a basic survival skill. And if there are lots of people choosing to hunt with a leader, that leader needs to be able to withstand all their scrutiny.

In the end, this is about values. People need to feel good about the leader's values. They need to believe that the leader's values are in sync with the organization's values and their own values. This is why getting the team's values incorporated into the burning imperative is so important. Just as people want to follow to an aspirational destination, they also want to follow someone they think of as a good person.

Best interests at heart: Of all the leader's values, the value the leader places on his or her followers is the most important to those followers. They want the leader to do well. And they want to share in the spoils of victory. If the leader is not going to share those spoils, eventually the followers will switch their allegiance to someone who will. People desperately need to believe the leader is watching out for them. So, it's really about the leader making it fun and sharing in the spoils of victory.

Judgment: Good intentions are never enough. Even if everyone shares the leader's mission, vision, and values, the leader and the team need to deliver. However they collectively define victory, the team must survive and win. And winning is about making the right choices with regard to strategy and tactics. The right choices come from good judgment. So followers, wanting to win, will follow a leader who knows what he or she is doing.

Judgments are made in each area of the P^3 framework: people, plans, and practices. This is about choosing and implementing the winning strategy, putting the right people in the right roles, and supporting them with the necessary enabling practices. The leader has to pick the right place to land, the right place to ford the stream, the right way to get across, the right people to build the bridge, and ensure that everyone else does his or her part getting to the early wins and eventually arrives at the aspirational destination. With that comes victory.

Followers first: Great leaders throughout history were more focused on their followers than they were on themselves. The more they were prepared to sacrifice for the benefit of their followers, the more loyal their followers were to them. These are the great legends in any culture, in any time. They're around today. They are easy to spot. They are the ones people are following.

Finis origine pendet (the end depends on the beginning) so says the Latin poet Manlius. In a transition into a new leadership role, if you do not get the beginning right, the end will be ugly. If you follow this book's framework and take advantage of its tools, you will be leading your team to the right place, in the right way, at the right times. If you do this, you will develop trust, loyalty, and commitment—and your team will follow. By using the proven onboarding methodologies presented in this book to enhance and synchronize your P^3 framework, you will build the tactical capacity required for you and your team to deliver better results faster than anyone thought possible.

Team, Marketing, and Strategic Planning Tools Useful across Steps

These appendices are team, marketing, and strategic planning tools and ideas that didn't quite fit into one of the main chapters but we thought some readers might find them useful at some point during their transition. Don't read them straight through, but pull them out as needed. Tools included are:

I Strategic Planning—An essential tool that fits into both the burning imperative and early wins. It's here because many readers already have their own way of doing this.

II SIPOC Tool—Useful in helping map out work flows.

III Decision Making Guidelines—Brief series of questions to inform tricky decisions.

IV Brand Positioning Tool—Foundational tool for marketing efforts.

V Creative Brief Tool—Foundational tool for managing creative work development.

VI Marketing Asset Management Tool—Great framework for thinking about sponsorships.

VII Partnerships/Alliances Guidelines—Clarifies make/buy/partner/license options.

VIII Strategic Map Tool—Way to visualize three dimensions in two.

IX Profit Pools Tool—Way to build an understanding of where the real value is in an industry.

Strategic Planning

Strategic planning is essential. It is the infrastructure for any winning business. If you are comfortable with the way you currently manage strategic planning, this is one of those sections you can skip or skim. However, there are some frameworks and definitions here that are useful for getting everyone in a new team on the same page.

Strategy is about the creation and allocation of resources to the right place in the right way at the right time over time. Strategic planning is about generating and selecting options. It is how the gaps between objectives and current reality are delineated, how resources are reassessed with a view to generating practical, immediate options to build the momentum to close those gaps. Strategic planning is tightly correlated to practical goals and concrete benchmarks for success. It is also bound up with building and executing the burning imperative that begins the program.

Development Process

You can think about strategy development in two steps:

1. Creating a set of strategic options and
2. Choosing which ones to pursue.

In the end, you are trying to come up with the best strategy to get you from your *current reality* to your *destination*. Unless you are already there, there is a *gap* between where you are and where you want to be. It is also likely that there are some *barriers* keeping that gap in place. The strategy in Figure AI.1 will guide your *actions* in bridging that gap.

We have drawn a two-dimensional figure to show that there are different possible routes to get from the current reality to the destination. Of course, it is really a multidimensional world with multiple routes. But sticking with the figure we've drawn, thinking in terms of a couple of dimensions helps create different options.

For example, if you were trying to increase sales, one dimension might be sales to existing customers. Another might be increasing the number of customers. You can increase total sales by moving along either dimension. Adding new customers might involve the action of recruiting sales "hunters" particularly adept at wooing new customers to overcome the barrier of not being able to contact enough customers. Increasing sales to existing customers might in-

FIGURE AI.I   Destination Planning

volve the action of recruiting client service "farmers" particularly adept at building deep relationships to overcome the barrier of not knowing enough about your current customers.

Leadership Involvement

One key idea is that you can help best if you fill dual roles during the process. Early on, acting as *coach*, you should provide input based on your experience to enhance scenarios and options and then improve valuation assumptions. At this point, you should not judge. Then, after all the assumptions are on the table and the valuations are done, acting as *manager*, you should make decisions. It is important for managers to judge, but not so early as to cut off expansive thinking. Coaches need to work hard to protect the ugly ducklings that might turn out to be swans (until it's time to drown them because they are not really swans, but just ugly).

How Strategic Planning Fits with Tactical Capacity

Tactical capacity is the bridge between strategic planning and implementation. When strategic planning clearly and coherently flows from the burning imperative and is incorporated by the team into their practices with a concrete appreciation of the "on the ground" reality it is then that tactical capacity—the ability to execute successfully—emerges.

A common mistake in companies and organizations is for strategic planning to be separated out from day-to-day business and to be imposed from above. Tactical capacity is about bringing the strategic plan—and the vision that drives it—into the day-to-day practices of the team. By building tactical capacity to reinforce strategic planning, a leader is assuring that the team will be able to perform decisively and astutely in unfamiliar circumstances.

Net Result

The net results of strategic planning are plans—strategic, action, resource, and performance management. Strategic planning, despite what many leaders think, can be and needs to be done quickly and efficiently. Furthermore, it must be done with a view to practical adoption and the collective sense of building tactical capacity.

Basic Steps

Here is a basic flow for strategic planning. It is a complete, robust planning process. Of course, different organizations will modify it to meet their needs. Some separate long-term planning from annual planning. Some use different processes for different organizations. We are not suggesting that this is the only way to do this. But it is a good way.

We are going to lay out the basic steps, explain them and then give you an example:

1. Set the aspirational *destination.*
2. Assess the facts of the *current reality* and develop future *scenarios.*
3. Identify *options* to bridge gaps between reality and aspiration.
   * Peer and management *input* to enhance scenarios and options.
4. *Evaluate* options under different scenarios.
   * Peer and management *involvement* to understand and improve valuation assumptions.
   * Management *agreement* on which options to pursue.
5. Develop detailed business *plans.*
6. *Act, measure, adjust,* and *repeat.*

Step I—Set the Aspirational Destination

Strategic planning begins with the aspirational long-term *destination,* which should look a lot like the vision in the burning imperative. It is important for this step to come before looking at the current reality. Starting with the current reality forces your team to build *from* the current existence which results in an incremental strategy that often leads a place far short of the aspirational destination. Starting with the end in mind, the aspirational destination allows the team to build a clear and direct path *toward* the aspiration.

Walt Disney did not set out to build a park of amusement rides that were incrementally better, he set out to create the "happiest place on earth."

Set your aspirational destination before you do anything else.

Step 2—Assess the Facts of the Current Reality and Develop Future Scenarios

The next step is to analyze the current reality. This involves a review, once again of the five Cs: customers, collaborators, capabilities, competitors, conditions as well as performing a SWOT (strengths, weakness, opportunities, threats) analysis.

Assessing the five Cs is the same process that you did during your due diligence phase but by now you should have far more insight and information than you did the first time you deployed this approach. For each of the five Cs, you want to assess the facts:

- What are the sources, drivers, and hinderers of revenue and value in the business (current and future)?
- Identify activities, costs, revenues, and profit pools by segment— for us and for the broadest possible universe of competition.
- Gather data on the end user/customer preference, commitment and price/value for both your company and the competition.
- Know the influencing external factors such as complementors, direct/indirect competitors, suppliers, regulatory issues, macro, and micro business environment.
- Where are the growth opportunities? Look for them by analyzing trends, and discontinuities, as well as the strengths and weaknesses of the current strategy.

The output from this process is a detailed SWOT analysis. To complete this, you can use the SWOT tool we provided earlier in this book (Tool 3.2 on p. 46). You may also want to do a capability balance sheet laying out your strengths and gaps across core competencies, assets, and processes:

Scenarios

Scenarios involve potential changes to the external world. They are generally outside the control of the organization. Given this, the organization cannot choose which one will happen, but it can lay out expected probabilities for each scenario happening. This is useful in terms of evaluating the expected results of different strategic options later.

Sustainable competitive advantages are really key leverage points that can continue to be leverage points under most of the future scenarios.

Sticking with the Disney example, one of the fundamental realities for Disney in Florida was that they were going to have to assemble a large tract of land that was currently in the hands of multiple landowners. Disney had money, but no local knowledge. The scenarios involved who found out what he was trying to do and when they found it out.

Step 3—Identify Options to Bridge Gaps between Reality and Aspiration

The basic question you should ask yourself is: Which strategic options might create additional value—or minimize its destruction? This is where creativity comes in as you come up with a range of options that could potentially address the issues and move the organization forward. For ideas, look hard at your key leverage points for offensive options and at your key business issues for defensive options.

This is a good time to get peer and management input into your thinking. You are trying to collect ideas. If peers or management has good ideas, you want to know about them. However, you are not looking for decisions yet, just input.

Some of Disney's options in Florida included buying the land himself, going through the local government and leveraging their rights of eminent domain, or buying the land through a third party behind the scenes.

Step 4—Evaluate Options under Different Scenarios

The question here is which strategic options create the most value over time, risk adjusted, under different scenarios? You'll want to evaluate options and scenarios leading to a range of forecasts based on transparent assumptions. At this point, the key stakeholders should become involved to understand and help improve the components of the valuation assumptions. Then, separately and later, you will want to get these key stakeholders involved to agree on which options to pursue.

Remember the three stakeholder points of involvement:

1. Input to enhance scenarios and options—capturing their ideas
2. Involvement to understand and improve valuation assumptions—tapping into their experience and context
3. Agreement on which options to pursue (which should fall out of the expected valuation of different options under different scenarios)

In Florida, Disney chose to engage outside companies to buy the various parcels of land, overcoming the barrier that prices would rise if people knew what he was trying to do. He chose not to try to assemble the land himself or in his own name or through the local government.

Step 5—Develop Detailed Business Plans

This is where you think through what strategic and operational actions are needed to implement each selected option:

- *Strategic plan:* Strategic posture (shape the industry of the future, adapt to the future, reserve right to play), resource allocation, rules of engagement across critical business drivers.
- *Action plan:* Actions, timetables, roles, responsibilities, linkages—for both immediate impact programs and capability enhancements.
- *Multiyear resource plan:* Human, financial, operational—requirements, application, sources.
- *Performance management plan:* Operating and financial performance standards, measures, and goals.

Step 6—Act, Measure, Adjust, and Repeat

Smith Kline Beecham had a very useful way of evaluating options. The steps they used are incorporated into the strategic planning tool just discussed. Done right, the choice of which option to pursue falls out of the scenario/option grid. Let's stick with our increasing sales example as an oversimplified way of showing this. Recall, the basic dimensions were increasing sales to existing customers (farming) or adding new customers (hunting).

Assume three scenarios for the future of the industry:

1. Industry consolidation—number of customers shrinking
2. Industry stagnation—number of customers constant
3. Industry expansion—number of customers increasing

To determine which of your strategic options (hunting, farming, or neither) has the highest expected value, you need to figure out what the payoff will be under each scenario and the probabilities of each happening.

Let's assume that hunters cost $100K each and generate $200K each in revenue in a period of expansion, $50K during stagnation and $25K during consolidation. Let's also assume that farmers cost $50K and generate $25K in a period of expansion, $40K during stagnation and $100K during consolidation. Looking at the options of adding either 10 hunters, adding 10 farmers, or adding nothing would produce a grid like this:

Profit Change ($000)		Expansion	Stagnation	Contraction
Add 10 hunters		1,000	−500	−750
Add none		0	0	0
Add 10 farmers		−250	−100	500
	Costs	**Revenue**	**Revenue**	**Revenue**
New hunter	100	200	50	25
Farmer	50	25	40	100

In a time of expansion, the best option is to add hunters so they can woo new market entrants. In a time of stagnation, the best option is to do nothing. In a time of contraction, the best option is to add farmers so they can capture existing customers' increasing market shares. It is easy to choose if you know what's going to happen. But if there is uncertainty as to which scenario will play out, the action choice is driven by the expected likelihood of each scenario.

If the bias is toward expansion, you might see something like this, leading us to add hunters:

Expansion Bias

Profit Change ($000)		Expansion	Stagnation	Contraction	Expected
Add 10 hunters		1,000	−500	−750	188
Add none		0	0	0	0
Add 10 farmers		−250	−100	500	−25
Probability (%)		50	25	25	
	Costs	**Revenue**	**Revenue**	**Revenue**	
New hunter	100	200	50	25	
Farmer	50	25	40	100	

Conversely, a contraction bias would look like this (adding farmers):

Contraction Bias

Profit Change ($000)		Expansion	Stagnation	Contraction	Expected
Add 10 hunters		1,000	−500	−750	−250
Add none		0	0	0	0
Add 10 farmers		−250	−100	500	163
Probability (%)		25	25	50	
	Costs	**Revenue**	**Revenue**	**Revenue**	
New hunter	100	200	50	25	
Farmer	50	25	40	100	

The different probabilities lead you to different choices. If you think the likelihood of expansion is greater, the expected value of the hunter focused option wins. If you think the likelihood of contraction is greater, you'll add farmers instead. Here we see the same scenarios, same options, same revenues and costs, but different choices. This is why it is so important to get everyone aligned around the assumptions.

Strategic Planning Summary

Strategic planning begins with the aspirational destination that is drawn from the vision and objectives from the burning imperative:

Analyze the *current reality* using the five Cs approach.

Complete a SWOT summary.

Create *strategy* options to guide *actions,* overcome *barriers,* and bridge *gaps.*

Get key stakeholder input into options and assumptions.

Get key stakeholder agreement on which strategic options to pursue.

Develop four key business plans:

1. Strategic plan
2. Action plan
3. Resource plan
4. Performance management plan

SIPOC Tool

Figure A (SIPOC) is a great, simple way to map work flows:

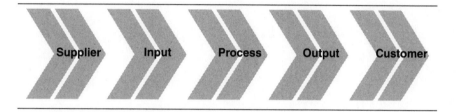

Suppliers provide inputs into the process.

Customers benefit from outputs of the process.

It is useful to map work flows for your team to understand these components.

Decision Tool

Sometimes the simplest tools are the most useful. This one consists of a brief series of questions to ask before making a tricky decision.

Have we examined the success rate of similar ventures?

Have we sought alternative viewpoints?

Have we asked for quantitative estimates of our chance of success?

Have we questioned the range of options with which we have been presented?

Brand Positioning

Often, it is going to be essential to clarify the brand positioning. This tool will help.

To (target audience), xxx is the brand of (frame of reference) that (emotional benefit point of difference) because (product/service/experience attributes).

Target

Who we're talking to (and not talking to)?

Should go beyond demographics to include psychographics, moods, occasions as appropriate.

Consumer versus Purchaser versus Influencer.

Bias to more narrow definitions.

Do we have a clear picture?

Affiliations? Interests?

Frame of Reference

Who we're competing against (and not competing against)?

If the target were to think about spending its time or money with us, but then chose to spend it somewhere else, where might that be?

Bias to broader category definitions.

Emotional Benefit Point of Difference

The different benefits that we provide.

In the end, all benefits are emotional, making the target feel differently. Is our point of difference believable/true?

Desired by the target? Preemptive? Emotional?

Product/Service/Experience Attributes

The attributes that deliver the point of difference/benefit.

Are they fact-based?

Do we have proof?

Is it enough to close the sale?

_____

_____

_____

_____

Total—Distinctive and different? Cohesive and complete?

Creative Brief Tool

This is one of the most valuable tools for accelerating creative work of any sort.

I Co-authored by the client and the agency teams—obsoletes the need for a separate creative brief document written subsequently inside the agency.

II Covers all the critical elements:

1. Project description (what is output—media types to be covered and timing for completion of each).
2. Positioning and brand character.
3. Competitive context.
4. Desired response (what do—aware, understand, believe, act):
   —Marketing objective
   —Communication strategy
5. Mandatory executional elements (visuals, selling idea).
6. Insight into target beliefs or practices (expressed best in actual customer/consumer language).

III Written in precision language. This means that every word on the page—just like every word in a poem—carries its own weight. Precision language is not only hard-working language; it is also honest language.

IV Signed off by the highest-ranking client and agency people responsible for the brand's communication to give it authority.

Marketing Asset Management Tool

This tool will help you think through what you want and what you're willing to give up to get it in the area of sponsorship.

Use for:

Multiyear investment commitments

Significant financial investments

High profile opportunities (publicity)

Unbudgeted opportunities

Description: What is the asset? What rights? What time period?

Fit: Business/brand strategy/target.

Activation plans: What getting done, by when, by whom

Benefits: Direct volume and profit, indirect volume and profit, brand preference, intangible benefits like goodwill.

Costs: Direct and indirect costs to acquire and activate.

Funding: Source (distributors, other divisions).

Accountability: How to measure and report

Three types of investments:

1. *Marketing assets:* A property, event, or environment that offers brand marketing value—grows brand equity and profitable volume.

    - Leverages meaningful consumer/customer context, environment, or theme.

- Has associate imagery that reinforces a brand's positioning.
- Has a target audience that reinforce a brand's positioning.
- Is activatable—Has brand building opportunities backed by a system commitment to fully exploit these.
- Has size (reach)/frequency of interaction consistent with brand needs.
- Satisfies the brand's seasonality or geographic priorities.

2. *Strategic availability accounts:* An account acquired to secure profitable volume.

3. *Constituent expenses:* Expenses incurred in order to influence the rights seller on other matters.

Partnerships/Alliances Guidelines

A simple tool to help clarify some choices.

Make: If creates ownable, valuable advantage

Buy: If can create more value faster than by making

Partner or license: If creates more value over time than can by owning

Strategic Map Tool

This tool is a way to visualize three dimensions in one- or two-dimensional space. If, for example, dimension 1 was market share and dimension 2 was customer segment and dimension 3 was profits, you might get a picture like this:

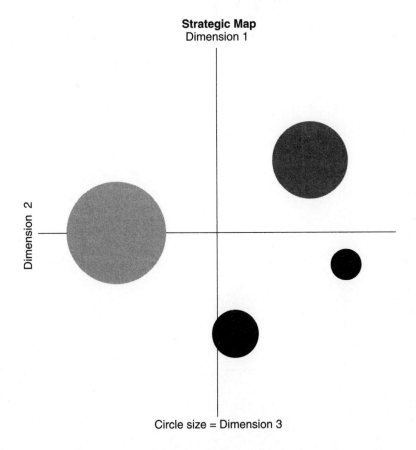

Strategic Map
Dimension 1

Dimension 2

Circle size = Dimension 3

Profit Pools Tool

Profit pool analysis is another useful tool for due diligence and situation analyses. It helps you visualize where the real money is in the industry. Those with sustainable competitive advantages should be able to capture a larger than normal share of the overall profit pool. As explained by Gadiesh and Gilbert,[1] this is an exercise in mapping all the profits of an industry. Lay out the operating margin for each component on one axis and the revenues on the other. The breadth and depth of profits by component are shown as:

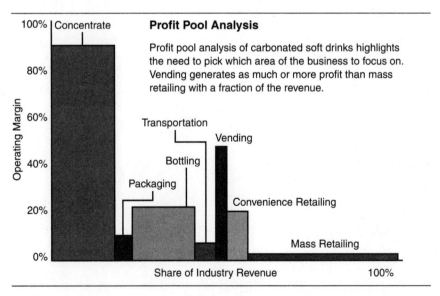

Profit Pool Analysis

Profit pool analysis of carbonated soft drinks highlights the need to pick which area of the business to focus on. Vending generates as much or more profit than mass retailing with a fraction of the revenue.

---

[1] Orit Gadiesh and James L. Gilbert, "A Fresh Look at Strategy,"*Harvard Business Review,* May 1998.

Buckingham, M., and Clifton, D. (2001). *Now Discover Your Strengths.* New York: Free Press.

Covey, S. (1989). *The Seven Habits of Highly Effective People.* New York: Simon & Schuster.

Duck, J. D. (2001). *The Change Monster.* New York: Three Rivers Press.

Eliot, T. S. (1943). "Little Giddings," *Four Quartets.* New York: Harcourt Brace Jovonovich.

Gadiesh, O., and Gilbert, J. L. (1998, May). A Fresh Look at Strategy. *Harvard Business Review.*

Gladwell, M. (2005). *Blink.* New York: Little, Brown.

Hilton, E. (2001). Differences in Visual and Auditory Short-Term Memory. *Indiana University South Bend Journal.*

Linver, S. (1984). *Speak and Get Results.* New York: Simon & Schuster.

Neff, T., and Citrin, J. (2005). *You're in Charge, Now What?* New York: Crown.

Senge, P. (1990). *The Fifth Discipline.* London: Century Business.

Smart, B. (1999). *Topgrading.* Upper Saddle River, NJ: Prentice-Hall.

Watkins, M. (2003). *The First 90 Days.* Boston: Harvard Business School Press.

George Bradt has a unique perspective on helping leaders move into complex, high stakes, new roles and accelerate transitions. After Harvard and Wharton, George spent two decades in sales, marketing, and general management around the world at companies including Lever Brothers, Procter & Gamble, Coca-Cola, and J. D. Power and Associates as chief executive of its Power Information Network spin off. Now he is managing director/CEO of PrimeGenesis, the executive on-boarding and transition acceleration group he founded in 2002. Since then, George and PrimeGenesis have reduced the risk of failure fourfold for new executives they've helped—from 40 percent to less than 10 percent. George can be contacted at gbradt@primegenesis.com.

Jayme A. Check is a proven leader with excellent motivational skills and a history of achieving results in traditional and entrepreneurial environments from Wall Street to Asia. He has broad-based experience in sales, business development, and strategy at Guidance Solutions, NHI Medical, Cape Enterprises, Brice Manufacturing, and J. P. Morgan. In addition to his role as one of the founding partners of PrimeGenesis, he is also the founder and current president of Quantum Leap Associates, a leadership and personal development firm focused on providing measurable results. Jayme earned a BS from Syracuse and an MBA from UCLA's Anderson School and can be contacted at jcheck@primegenesis.com.

Jorge Pedraza transitioned from a career as a professor at Williams College to working in start-up environments at Concrete Media, Guidance Solutions, and Le Monde Interactive. At Williams, Jorge was known for his excellent thinking and teaching and his active involvement in college governance at the most senior levels. He then turned these talents to helping organizations figure out how to leverage the Internet to reinvent themselves. His most recent venture has been to help found Unison Site Management, a specialty finance company focused on wireless telecommunications where he has helped turn a business concept and a blank piece of paper into a company with 100 employees and over $300 million in assets in less than three years. Jorge has a BA from Cornell and a doctorate from Yale and is one of the founding partners of PrimeGenesis. He can be contacted at jorge.pedraza@primegenesis.com.